WINNIPEG
JUL 2 6 2010
JUL 20 2010
PUBLIC LIBRARY

Journeycakes:

Memories With My Antiguan Mama

D1292175

Journeycakes:
Memories With My Antiguan Mama
BY MONICA MATTHEW

Copyright © 2008 by Monica Matthew

All rights reserved. No portion of this book may be reproduced, stored in a retrieval system, or transmitted in any form or by any means — electronic, mechanical, photocopy, recording, scanning, or other — except for brief quotations in critical reviews or articles, without the prior written permission of the publisher and/or author. For additional information contact:

Grays Farm Publishing
Church Street Station
P. O. Box 1926
New York, NY 10008

Paperback ISBN-13: - 978-0-615-18206-3
Paperback ISBN-10: 0-615-18206-2

Grays Farm Publishing
Manufactured in the United States of America
www.journey-cakes.com
Copyright © 2008 Monica Matthew
All rights reserved.

ISBN: 0-615-18206-2
ISBN-13: 9780615182063

Visit www.booksurge.com to order additional copies.

Journeycakes:

Memories With My Antiguan Mama

By Monica Matthew

Grays Farm Publishing
New York City
www.journey-cakes.com

To the ancestors who left the indelible mark of parenting.
To Mama May, all mothers, grandmothers,
and others who love and nurture children.
To the future generations who have never known the beauty of
Mama May Ambrose, this book is my gift to you.

— Monica Matthew

Wisdom has built her house;
she has hewn out its seven pillars.
She had prepared her meat and mixed her wine;
she has also set her table.
She has sent out her maids and she calls
from the highest point of the city.
"Let all who are simple come in here!"
she says to those who lack judgment.
"Come eat my food
and drink the wine I have mixed.
Leave your simple ways and you will live;
walk in the way of understanding."

— Proverbs 9:1-6 (NIV)

Preface

Who goes to a funeral and brings home a child? Mama May, born Mary Ambrose.

When my mother Ruth died in 1956, Mama May, who came only to pay respect to the dead, reached to take me from my father's extended arms. I was a nineteen-month-old girl.

"Miss May," he said, "take care ah this little girl for me."

For the next twenty-odd years, I experienced a quality of love and parenting that I wish to share with you here.

Mama's philosophy about child rearing was simple: "Children are blessings from heaven," and, as her grandmother had taught her as early as 1924, "be devoted to de children God put in yuh care."

Over the years, I have often wondered if I have told my children enough about Mama May. I have told them stories about her work, the lessons she taught, the ways she loved in silence. I have told my daughter, Monifa, how Mama May banded my abdomen with cloth after I gave birth, which restored my small waistline. Mama instilled in me, her adopted daughter, important life lessons. These lessons were taught with love, and were shared in happy times, during conflicts, during difficult challenges, through personal grief and sacrifices. In the presence of folly, she was always wise. My children have all heard Mama's proverbial quotations, which I have instinctively hurled at them over time. Mama's axioms have become mine. Her legacy is now theirs.

Although I was not her biological child, there was a love affair between us, like a true mother and daughter. That love could not have been greater if she had delivered me from her own womb. In 2001 as she lay in her hospital bed following a stroke surrounded by family, I felt a compelling urge to tell of this love. I wanted to relate more about this great woman to my own children, to the family who sat at her bedside, to the grandchildren and great grandchildren waiting back at her house, to those loved ones who were abroad; they all needed to hear about her special journey.

To the young and those yet to be born, I want Mama May to be a reference, a historical monument in their minds and hearts, so that the tendency to forget our past will end. The goodness, the perseverance, the commitment, and the rich ancestral legacy of love for their heritage must be remembered forever through Mama May.

I am now part of that legacy: a legacy Mama's grandmother first shared with her. The woman Mama became, and some of what I have become, sprouted from past generations of love and parenting, from dedication and devotion to children and to family, or, in Mama's own words, "... de children God put in yuh care."

In writing this memoir, I have often felt driven not by my own volition, but by the will of the ancestral spirits. The powers of Mama May, Sophie Daniel (her grandmother), Annie Jacob (my maternal grandmother), Lesroy Walker (my grandfather), Ruth and Daniel Tittle (my biological parents), and the many others who had shown love and commitment by their deeds, are all a part of that drive. They are among my ancestors, who have survived against all odds, and thrived despite the horrors of the Middle Passage, the enslavement and drudgery of plantation life, and the loss of their African identity.

— *Monica Matthew*

Author's Acknowledgments

I am blessed by the quality of people God has allowed to enter my life during the process of writing this book. Beverly Benjamin George has been the push behind the birth of this book. In the early part of my writing, the late Martin Simmons was instrumental in choreographing my remembrance of my childhood memories. The Antigua and Barbuda International Literary Festival allowed me to read at the festival in 2007 before the book was published. Byron Patrick Tittle contributed the poem about Mama; thank you, Byron. My children, Chiqui and Monifa, have always believed that I could do this and have given literary support and moral encouragement. Author and friend, Joanne C. Hillhouse, the book's editor, aided in its improvement. Patricia Becker made invaluable suggestions. My sister Daisy James was a resourceful family historian.

I am thankful to family and friends: the Tittles, my brother Dunstan, the Walkers, Eileen, Gloria, Avril, Elizabeth, Dudley and Charlesworth. Many thanks to my grandchildren, Khadeejah, Yahya, and Ahmad who continue to ask questions about Mama May.

Lastly, to my colleagues at the Allen Stevenson School, Deirdre, Christaline, Charles, Nancy, Andy, Stephen, and the boys and teachers of the Lower School, who listened to my stories about Mama May, year after year. I was always encouraged.

CHAPTER ONE

Mama in Hospital in 2001

".... be devoted to de children God put in yuh care."

"What you think? Think Mama in pain?" Andy asked. "Ah don't want her to feel any pain; ah don't want her to suffer."

Andy was my thirty-seven-year-old cousin and the second of Mama's seventy-five grand and great grandchildren. The two of us were standing vigil at Mama's bedside at the Holberton Hospital in Antigua. The year was 2001 and I was forty-six years old.

Andy's show of emotion captured my attention for I had grown up in Antigua where I had seldom seen men reveal this depth of emotion. Generally, Antiguan men were not socialized to be open with their feelings; rather, it was considered manly to hide behind inexpressive and distant looks. Men like my uncle, Daddy Edmund, my father's brother and the father of Mama's eight children, and Grandpa Cubana, Mama's own father, demonstrated little emotional attachment to anyone or anything. I had never seen either of them cry. On the other hand, Antiguan women in my neighbourhood openly cried at funerals, screamed during fights with their spouses, and visibly suffered when a child became sick. I was pleased to see my cousin now candidly showing his emotions.

I knew that Mama had planted those seeds of love in Andy years ago. I witnessed the situation from the beginning, when I was a young girl. In 1964, Mama's second daughter, Elaine, migrated to the Virgin Islands and left her ten-month-old son in Mama's care. Because Andy was plagued with asthma, Mama searched for a homemade remedy to tame the monster that inhabited his lungs and made him struggle for air. To calm his wheezing, Mama often prepared a salve of nutmeg mixed with a soft candle melted on brown paper, which she would wrap around his chest. It was an anxious time for all of us in the house when he had an asthma attack. Sometimes I would breathe in deeply with him, as if that would increase oxygen to his lungs.

Occasionally, a gut-wrenching plea to God would arise from Mama: "Have mercy, Lord. Please help me with this pickney." I would hear her scream this from across the narrow hallway, followed quickly by the shuffling of feet and rustling of clothes as she rushed him to this same hospital. Each time she left, I wondered if the monster would win and Mama would return to the house without Andy.

When Andy entered his teenage years, he was no longer asthmatic. We all believed that it was Mama who killed the monster, that the folk remedies tried over the years — lizard head soup, cattle tongue tea, inflammation bush, burned incense, Ferrol, Codol, Scotch emulsion, cod liver and shark oils—were what healed him.

Standing now at her bedside, it was clear that Andy had been greatly affected by Mama's nurturing. "You think Mama in pain?" he repeated more faintly. I did not know what to say. I yearned for an answer, an answer to comfort the two of us.

As we watched Mama lying there, unresponsive except for a moaning sound coming from deep within her chest, the words spoken earlier by the staff nurse lingered in my head. I had driven straight from the airport to the hospital and listened attentively as she briefed me about Mama's stroke and the complications of her diabetes.

"Ms. Mary Ambrose is not her best now. Don't expect too much, as she comes and goes," the nurse said. The woman's face had hung solemnly. In her formality, she had reminded me that Mama's actual name was Mary. It was a name seldom used because it was not until Mama was forty years old that she discovered, when applying for a passport, that she was "Mary," not "May."

I searched the nurse's face for some hope that Mama was not fatally ill. I expected some sign of empathy, sympathy, or concern. The face gave back nothing. Training must have changed over the years, I thought. I scurried away from her to find Mama.

Magetson Ward was lined with beds along the entire length of an oblong room. A faint whiff of Gentian Violet, pine, and iodine stirred memories in me of past visits to this hospital. There was a mixture of emotions and memories: teenage pleasure and shock when I was kissed by the radiologist after he took an x-ray of my lower abdomen, or the safety and serenity I felt, when years later I enjoyed expert care during the birth of my children Chiqui and Monifa, with Mama present at the bedside. But the recollections also included inoculations with blunt needles, made so by repeated boiling and reuse, the screams of children frightened by the sight of the place, and, too often, the rough attention given them by the medical personnel. During the '70s, liquid medicines would only be issued to patients who brought a bottle with them to the hospital dispensary. Now, thirty years later, the unwashed walls, hard-backed chairs, and overall gloom on transient faces made me realize that the conditions had worsened. Modernity had been delayed.

I moved quickly through Magetson Ward to the casualty section. A line of beds stretched around the oblong room, each bed populated by an old woman. Some were fidgeting feebly with pieces of clothing or wrappings of brown paper; others were simply too ill to be alert. A few heads were tied with madras cloths, with an occasional gray braid dangling lifelessly alongside a gaunt face.

As my eyes and heart searched for familiarity, one of the women wearing a madras head tie surprised me with the strength and clarity of her voice.

"You looking for Miss May?" the woman said. As she raised her head in my direction, I saw a wiry, wrinkled neck and lips spread over a protruded chin.

"Yes, ma'am," I answered, wondering how she had come to that conclusion. She nudged the chin towards the corner of the room and extended her lips.

"She right on de other side. Most ah the people come visit this ward, come to her."

I turned in the direction indicated and saw a bottle of Alcolado Glacial rub standing all alone on the night table by Mama's hospital bed. The scarcity of personal belongings struck me. It made me wonder if old people hated hospital stays for this reason. At home things were different for Mama. Pictures of family lined the walls, a pile of Search-A-Word books lay on the couch nearby, and always within arm's reach were brown paper bags filled with bread, buns, crackers, mangoes, or sugar apples ready to be shared.

But even here, under a thin, over-washed, white hospital sheet, was something very familiar to me. It was the part of Mama's silhouette that had been permanently etched in my mind: a prominent high stomach that defied weight loss, ageing and laxatives. It protruded as if she had swallowed a watermelon. As a young girl, it was my responsibility to fit Mama into her chosen attire for special outings. Like a common laborer, I pulled and tucked, determined to tame that torso with a girdle, but at most, shaving only an inch or two away. Now, I gently caressed the belly we had barely flattened back then.

Mama's eighty-one-year-old face was round and sprinkled with tiny warts. Her slightly slanted eyes, smooth dark complexion, and thin pouting lips came together to depict an African elder. There was also a quiet aura about her as she lay there. I felt that Mama was separated from me not only physically, but also mystically, as if she were a queen lying in state or floating on a river outside an ancient city.

A swell of pride reminded me that I held a prized position in Mama's heart, and I felt certain that if she could hear me she would be all right. I thought, Mama needs to know I am here. She has been waiting for me to come.

"Mama, it's me, Monica," I said. "I'm here. I have come Mama."

Tears blinded my eyes as I continued to speak, hopeful that wherever her spirit had journeyed as a result of the stroke, the love between us was strong enough to bring her back. My eyes and hands surveyed the length of her still, stout body. How could Fate allow this? Mama, a thoroughbred, had raced through life in constant motion. She had raised not only her offspring, but many grandchildren, great-grandchildren, and other children she adopted. Through it all, she worked, cooked, and taught. To her the race was for the swift and the ones who could endure. I wanted Mama to endure.

Mama was born in 1920 on Gray's Farm Road. Her caring for others began shortly thereafter when she developed a strong bond with her grandmother. It continued through the birth of her first child in 1939, and lasted right up until this sudden, unfamiliar hospital stay. Such a long journey should have been reason enough to accept the end, but I could not. Looking closely now, as she lay in hospital unresponsive, I knew age would never be reason enough to relinquish her to death. Mama had taught me that in every situation, love was strongest: love brought hope and love erased fear. Mopping her brow and patting her hair—now as white as coconut meat—I spoke to her again.

"I love you Mama. Oh my Mama May, I love you so much. It's Monica. Mama, let me know that you hear me, squeeze my hand, smile, give me some sign Mama," I pleaded. Mama cannot leave yet, I told myself.

For a moment I reminded myself of life's inevitable changes. Wasn't I being unreasonable? Most of Mama's adult friends and family members — Cousin Chrissy, Mr. Norris, Mr. Mack, Miss Doris, Miss Freda, and so many others — had all died. Mama had outlived some by twenty years. Yet, this did not change my expectation. I believed in my heart that if she only knew I was here, it would make all the difference, and that wherever Mama was on this spiritual journey, she could be reached because I loved her deeply.

It was during all this reflection that Andy arrived and posed his question about Mama's pain. He needed words to ease his fear, and must have thought that I needed some too.

"Ah gave her porridge just dis morning; Mama sit up and talk and I cleaned her up," he said. I smiled inwardly; he had cleaned and dressed Mama!

I held Mama's hands, the same hands that had often held mine to cross the street, or write the alphabet. The dark rough skin, decorated with fine lines, was the result of years of work at the Antigua Sugar Factory, cooking for the workmen in the high season and pounding stones in the off-season. The knuckles, now slightly bent from arthritis, had washed hundreds of tubs packed with clothes and offered many meals to neighbours. Mama used her hands to teach me how to hem a dress, to iron a blouse, and to change a baby's diaper.

Before all of this, however, these hands had reached out to take me from my father's extended arms when I was nineteen months old. The year was 1956 and I was at my mother's funeral in St Phillip's village.

I still do not know if Mama had expected such an offer on that day. Who plans to take a child after the dead have been buried? Mama, and Elaine, along with my Uncle Edmund had traveled by bus from Gray's Farm village. Their other six children were left at the house, the youngest, Fitzroy, barely two and half years old. A neighbour likely said to her, "Go Miss May, ah will have an eye on them fu you."

I imagine the scene with my father and Mama May in his two roomed concrete flat. He might have thought about the moment since the previous night. His words were casual: "Miss May, take care ah dis little girl for me." There might have been some delay in Mama's response, for she had come only to pay respect to the dead. Mama's house in Gray's Farm only had two bedrooms, and she might have reminded herself that seven young mouths were already there to be fed and cared for.

I often wondered why she decided to take me. Each of my siblings—Yvonne, Eardley, Dunstan, and Eunette—presented a better option. Yvonne, the oldest, could wash, cook and clean. Eardley could fill a large container with water, sweep the yard, and feed the pigs. Dunstan and Eunette could dress themselves. That left my two-days-old sister Avril and me. Mama knew well the work involved in raising another small child. One who, at nineteen months, had some awareness of existence. At that age, a child knows her mother, her smell and sound, the taste of her skin as she crawls and clings to her mother's legs. A child that age would have adapted to the house, knowing when to turn corners to avoid a mahogany chest or how far to wander to the front door as she curiously surveyed the expanse of a tiny flower garden. At least baby Avril had little emotional attachment. Yet, even knowing this, Mama May consented to my father's wish.

That day, when all paternal obligations passed from my father's hands, he might not have cried. Experience told me he would have hid his tears. "Be strong," Mama told her sons, "No woman should see you cry."

Perhaps in my father's heart there was an iota of comfort. He had known Mama for years and had witnessed her strength as she raised the many children she had borne for his brother Edmund. My father had sensed love from this woman and perhaps felt it could be shared with his child. Perhaps instinct told him a child needed a certain kind of love to survive.

Avril would succumb to death in a few months. A young fruit plucked too early from her mother.

Taking my few belongings, Mama may have looked back at the children who remained, and wished she could take more. "This is not a man's role," were her thoughts all the way back to Gray's Farm, as she hugged me close to her bosom.

Over the ensuing years, Mama offered various explanations for my father's circumstances:

"It was tough you know; his wife was only thirty-three, young and loving."

"He worked hard in the fields then came home to care and fuss with children."

"His heart eventually gave up."

My sister Yvonne remembered that my father played dominos frequently at the corner, under the street lights, late into the night, possibly to escape the grief.

Two years later, Mama returned to that same house to attend my father's funeral. She left with my brother, Eardley, to bring him to join the children God placed into her care.

As I sat alongside Mama's hospital bed, I thought that she must continue on as a part of my life. I wanted her to be on the phone when I was sick and aching, or to share stories about the times when she was young. I needed her to remind me that maiden blush bush was good for a woman's abdominal problems, that cerasse and green papaya cured high blood pressure, and that evening primrose oil and red clover leaves soothed hot flashes. I wanted my grandchildren to know her as their great-grandmother. I wanted her to stay alive to remind me how to rub their navels with lamp oil for colic, and how to apply nutmeg mixed with a soft candle on brown paper for a wheeze. I expected her to remain lucid and be engaged with the children in her house at Cassada Gardens. I wanted her to be lasting because, in my heart, I knew she was the last sinew keeping the family together.

As I stood there caressing Mama May, I became aware for the first time of her vulnerability. She had not been hospitalized since 1960 when she gave birth to twins, Barrymore and Patmore. The previous delivery of her fifth child, Ira, had been the most painful of all her childbirths. His shoulder wanted to come first and the midwife had to maneuver and maneuver until he was in a less dangerous position.

I could not recall Mama ever being ill. Her only complaints were "the old pains" in her back, knees, and shoulders. I would use Benjamin's Healing Oil, Radiant B, or mustard cream, and my left hand to rub her aches; she believed a left-hander was more effective in ridding the body of pain.

"Use de left hand, then knock ah piece of wood to transfer the pain," she would say.

Growing up, Mama had strange ways to declare her strength.

"I'm an hombre! Don't mess with me," she often said.

Mama stood five feet, two inches tall, and weighed about 165 pounds. She was not intimidated by anyone. Before I learned that hombre was the Spanish word for man, I thought it meant that at anytime, she could morph into a huge, hideous creature. Frequently, she would say, "I'm a hard 'tone woman," referring to the presence of male genitalia. It was uttered with such conviction that I occasionally wondered whether it might be possible.

The day I realized the meaning of those words, I asked, "Mama, whe' you get 'tone from?"

"Never mind," she laughed, "you not to use that word anyhow."

But now I know it was simply about status. Society treated men differently, this she knew. She had felt it, and she had seen it, too. Women lost jobs in the civil service if they became pregnant and were unmarried, while unmarried men in the civil service frequently fathered children, very often with several women. The wage in her weekly envelope was never equal to that of the men with whom she worked at the sugar factory. A declaration of 'hombre' put Mama on equal standing with the father of her children, Edmund Tittle, or with her own father, Joseph Ambrose.

For an hour or so Andy and I stood at Mama's bedside as the nurse came by to check her vital signs. The gurgling sound coming from Mama dropped in volume then picked up in frequency with the rise and fall of her high abdomen. I feared that sound. Growing up in Gray's Farm around old folks, there had been many conversations about that sound after someone died.

"Ah tell you he won't last, you hear dat sound he mek last night? That ah de sound ah death."

By the end of visiting hours, a sea of family members stood in vigil. They had come from all corners of Antigua: some from Mama's house at Cassada Gardens, some from Gray's Farm Road, and more were on the way from New York. They stood around Mama like a brood of chickens around a mother hen, one who on so many previous occasions had stood over them. She had stood waiting for a fever to break. She had stood peering at a newborn grandchild and pointing out a family trait — "That child has the Tittle hairy hand and foot," or "You see how he toe lap over the other, de pittance of Tittle family," or "Ah me father nose that, he's a true Ambrose."

She had taken swollen legs into her lap to nurse bulbous cysts, squeezing out yellow and bloody pus to ease the fever and pain. She had treated tender lymph nodes with hot compressors, slapped a warm roasted potato on mumps, and applied hot aloes to feet infected by rusted nails or sliced open by broken glass. She had attended christenings, confirmations, graduations, weddings, and funerals. Looking around the hospital now at the many cheerless faces, I knew we were all drawn here because we had benefited from Mama's journey, from her reign as queen. She had reigned supremely for over seventy years. Assembled together, we solemnly watched, hoped and prayed.

That night, I drove from the hospital to Gambles Terrace, a quiet, residential neighborhood just outside of the city. As I settled in for the evening, I dreaded hearing the ring of the telephone. "Ms. Jacob has turned for the worse." That was what the nurse had said when my maternal grandmother, Annie Jacob was sick in 1977. "Turn for the worse " was the expected phrase when the elderly entered hospital in Antigua; they were not expected to return home. I was not ready to hear such news about my Mama May.

Early the next morning, my sister-friend Gloria prepared hot arrowroot porridge. She handed me a flask of the porridge and said, "The nutmeg in the porridge is good for stroke; try to get her to eat some." I set out for the hospital once again with an eerie feeling. There was no way to prepare myself for such a visit.

The morning air was perfumed with hibiscus, and yellow bells. There were ominous signs as well. A dog howled across the street, which intensified my fear. It is a common belief in Antigua that dogs howled when someone was about to die. Fifteen minutes later, as I neared the hospital compound, a flock of blackbirds hovered overhead. Blackbirds were another bad sign from my childhood. They were not to be stoned, because they were the dead reincarnated. Children would say to each other, "Never point you finger at a blackbird." If someone did, we would instruct the person to "bite each finger and pray that dem no rotten off."

I entered the hospital and found the Magetson Ward. A clock that hung crookedly in the hallway ticked loudly. The nurse's desk was empty. I found myself missing the nurse, and her ritual debriefing. I was fearful, yet the unexpected made me brave. Gathering strength for the possibility that Mama had taken a turn for the worse, I pushed open the double doors to the ward.

Immediately, I sensed something ethereal, like someone was staring at me. The glare was coming from the direction of Mama's bed.

"Mama?" I exclaimed in shock.

Looking a little bewildered, Mama sat propped up in bed, quite upright, as if she were on her sofa back at Cassada Gardens, surrounded by all her familiar things.

It was unbelievable! I rushed towards her bedside, and as I kissed and kissed her over and over again, I cried.

I had not noticed Andy right away. But now his flash of white teeth, a smile spreading from ear to ear, and his joyful tears were welcomed sights. My attention, though, was on Mama. She had indeed changed. It was not a turn for the worse, but a change for the better.

She tried to speak, "Monica, dey say...." She tried again, syllables dotted with pauses. Some words were inaudible, some reversed in a sentence. Tears ran down her face. I could see the frustration on her face. She pointed at the Bible, and I read Psalm 91, her favorite scripture. All the while, I was gratefully thanking God for Mama's improvement. The majestic aura was still there and again I felt a spiritual presence; perhaps it was an Angel of Life hovering over the bed.

Mama spent the rest of the week in hospital. Her oldest daughter Elaine and her granddaughter, Andrea, arrived from New York with other grand and great-grandchildren. We all witnessed Mama's anxiety as she struggled to communicate her thoughts, her thin lips pouting, and tears flowing soundlessly when she was not understood. Several days out of hospital, the miracle continued. Family and friends arrived, children fussed and screamed, and Mama's voice joined in the fray. Children were always her source of energy. We joked that she had waved her scepter to summon her subjects. To this, she smiled gracefully, relishing the influence she possessed.

Slowly, Mama returned to her old routine. She would sit perched on a flowered sofa, her stocky legs slightly bent from arthritis, a bag filled with money and personal documents within arm's reach, and a few packages of crackers, bread, and cookies at hand to distribute to the children. She kept a few mangoes ripening in a brown paper bag sitting under a chair; and occasionally the sweet cooing of her laughter would fill the room.

This illness was the catalyst that brought an end to her independence and hands-on involvement in the lives of those still living with her. Although the visible signs of Mama's stroke disappeared, we all knew that life as we knew it would change. Of course Mama could not understand it all. She could not understand because her existence was tied to the young. Over the years she had cared for one generation after the other. Babies had belted out protesting screams as she held them and sucked a nostril blocked by mucous. They bit her fingers as she cleaned mouths infected with thrush. Her reign had ended, or at best was interrupted.

I had to prepare myself once again to leave Mama.

Ira, Mama's son, made arrangements for a caregiver. A few days later, I stopped in to see her before boarding a flight for New York. Joyce, the caregiver was nearby. I could see in Mama's eyes some resistance to this new situation, and was certain no one would replace this Queen Mary in her own house, stroke or not.

As I left Antigua that day, I thought about Mama May in hospital the day of my arrival, about the outpouring of love from her children, and about the passing of reins. I had an intense desire to recapture her life, to revisit the time when she was young and active, when she ran like a racehorse beating the odds, caring for three generations of the young and the old simultaneously. It was a desire that would consume me for some time.

CHAPTER TWO

The Grandmother, Sophie

"Learn To Be Responsible & Tek Care Ah Yuh Business"

"My Grandie was the only person dat love me back then," Mama said, with certainty.

Her grandmother, Sophie Daniel, was a continuous presence in Mama's life from her birth in 1920 to her fifteenth birthday. Left in Sophie's care by her parents before she was four years old, Mama found her grandmother to be as doting towards her, the first granddaughter, as any mammal with a newborn. Sophie's own four children were adults by 1925, so she was happy to have a small girl in the midst, and quickly added Mama to the "...children God put in yuh care."

Sophie's love and commitment to her granddaughter paralleled those in my own life with Mama. When Mama May took me into her home, she was doing what her grandmother had done thirty-five years earlier.

Deprived of a mother and father by four years of age, she would snuggle into Sophie's back at night as they slept in the same bed. There was never a kiss or a hug when she did, nor did Sophie ever speak of love. It was not customary to say "I love you" to children in those days. But Mama knew her grandmother loved her very much.

"I was the spoilt child for my grandmother Sophie, and I called her Grandie," Mama, proclaimed with pride. "My grandmother used to cook whatever I want to eat, even if she had to put two pots on de fire." Sophie felt a little nurturing was in order and believed that spoiling could not do much harm. She knew Mama was forlorn over her mother's absence and hoped a grandmother's love would counter the trauma. Sophie knew she could succeed at this because she herself had been cared for by parents who loved her. As Mama May's grandmother tried to satisfy the young girl's yearning for her own parents, the bond between them became unbreakable.

Sophie was born in Seaton's Estate and had moved to Gray's Farm as a young woman. In those days, Sophie was a farmer who used to walk for miles from Gray's Farm to Hermitage Estate to dig for potatoes, pick cotton, or weed land leased from white owners. At that time, there was still a colonial system of estate servitude in Antigua, tied directly to sugar production where a syndicate owned the land, post emancipation. Antiguan blacks, like those of other British West Indian territories in the Caribbean Sea, had been liberated from slavery in the 1830s, but found their circumstances largely unchanged one hundred years later. Land was either leased to small farmers or people were employed to work on the estates, receiving very little income in return. Sophie would stretch the few shillings and pence from her weekly wage and coupled with money she occasionally received from Mama's parents, who were abroad, she was able to purchase a plot of land and build her own home in Gray's Farm village. This was the same piece of land on which Mama May built her home years later, and to this day remains in the family.

Sophie planted the first seed of self-esteem in Mama's head when she said to her one day, "From now on you name Miss May. Tell you friends. Any big people call you May, tell dem you Grandie Sophie say you name Miss May." Imagine at the age of eight, in 1928, an ordinary child growing up in Gray's Farm being addressed as "Miss." It was Sophie's intention to instill high expectations, self-esteem and dignity in this female child.

Sophie never whipped Mama, not once! This was unheard of in a West Indian household. Parents stuck to the Bible's instruction to "spare the rod and spoil the child." But Sophie had been part of estate living; she had been beaten. She had told Mama that her own mother was born into slavery, and had been beaten also. Therefore Sophie consciously departed from tradition and spared Mama the embarrassment of corporal punishment, though others in Mama's life would act differently.

One Friday, twelve-year old Mama came home from school for lunch and was met at the door of the large one bedroom wooden house by Sophie.

"Miss May, me have no lunch to ghee you t'day," she said. To Mama, there was no reason to think that her grandmother was joking. There had been many times of shortage: no meat on the dinner plate, an empty food safe, sometimes only a piece of a loaf of bread, gutted up and stuffed with sugar or nothing at all. During those lean times, when the young girl protested, Sophie would say, "Miss May, me say mek out; be content wid wha you get." This time around, fear of another day without lunch incited rebellion.

Mama took off. As she herself explained, "all the way to Five Islands, ah take off with one running." She knew her aunt, Sophie's daughter, Sue, would have ground provisions and that fresh fish would be there the next morning. Mama had not notified anyone of where she was going, and did not return until the next day, Saturday morning. Sophie, and Mama's father Joseph Ambrose (known to all as Grandpa), were worried sick, and were extremely angry even though she returned with a wooden box on her head carrying some sweet potatoes, yams, cassava and few small fish.

"Grandie Sophie didn't lift a finger to hit me; she only run her mouth," Mama boasted to me. But her son had to be appeased: so Sophie watched and cringed at every lash he landed on his daughter's back in punishment.

The strong bond between Mama and Sophie never faltered, even when Sophie destroyed something dear to her. Mama had received a doll from Aunt Sue who had since migrated to America.

Sophie, with good intentions, wrapped the doll in newspaper and stored it away for safekeeping. Months later, when she retrieved the doll to give it to Mama, baby roaches were crawling out of the eyes. Mama expressed how angry she was.

"Ah so vex, me just dig a hole and bury de dolly."

The hardships of the 1930's permeated every household across Antigua, especially in the villages where sugar cane and farming were the main sources of work. Wages were menial and people were hungry. Sophie must have made sacrifices in raising her own children, and Mama May as well.

Mama fondly remembered a pair of knitted sandals Sophie bought from the one of the Arab storeowners in St. John's city. It was a privilege, for many of Mama's peers went to school without shoes. There was even a new school dress for the contented young girl.

Providing an education was a priority to Sophie. And though she herself had no formal schooling, Sophie told Mama that education was the only way to leave the fields of hard work and low wages from the backra—the colloquial term for the white man. Mama had expressed a desire to teach. When other young girls had either started their own families or had entered the work force to help with the economic difficulties at home, Sophie encouraged Mama to stay in school. She saw potential in her granddaughter and often reminded her that the Ambroses, Mama's paternal relatives, were bright people. When Mama's schoolwork earned top points for spelling, math and writing, Sophie would boast about her granddaughter's academic ability.

"Hey, hey, you people dem ah bright people. You have dem brain, Miss May." Sophie smiled from ear to ear when Mama passed Seventh Standard Examination, the test required to complete formal schooling in those days. Strutting round the yard proud as a chanticleer, she crowed to the neighbours,

"Miss May parse Seventh Standard, ah tell you de Ambrose an dem ah bright people." Mama was always happy to please her grandmother too.

But as doting as Sophie was, she never lost the opportunity to teach lessons of life. When Mama's hormones were stirring throughout her body and boiling to a level of adolescent rebellion, although Sophie understood, she was still determined to show Mama that she was a strong disciplinarian.

"Ah won't tek no nonsense from you Miss May," Sophie would say.

For years Sophie had been washing and cooking, giving her now fourteen-year-old granddaughter the freedom to study her schoolwork and learn sewing instructions twice a week from one of the local seamstresses. Though such practices put Mama apart from other girls, Sophie intended to keep the young woman grounded and responsible.

"My grandmother used to wash my clothes. One day, my grandmother call me over as she stoop over de wash tub. A helluva pin was sticking out her middle finger," Mama said.

Sophie reminded her, "Ah warn you once before, Miss May. From now on, wash you own clothes." Sophie was slowly relinquishing her roles.

Not long after, Mama was cooking her own meals because of a comment she made about Sophie's cooking. That day, Mama remarked that "dis rice nah taste good 'tall, Grandie." She had wanted to say this many times before, when there wasn't any oil in the rice, or maybe no onion, or not enough fat meat to deliver flavor, but she knew that her grandmother struggled daily to make ends meet.

Sophie was offended by the remarks.

"You forward, Miss May. From now on cook you own food too." But Mama did not mind; it was a special moment to watch her grandmother "cut and contrive" by portioning small amounts of ingredients to her. She liked the taste of independence. Perhaps Sophie in her wisdom felt it was time for Miss May to "learn to be responsible and tek care ah you business."

"It was some hard times then," Mama explained to me. It was 1935, the depression was going on in America, a world war was brewing, and there was a drought in Antigua. Hardship was felt in all the Caribbean islands and unemployment was high. People were hungry. The Moyne Commission was set up by the British government to analyze the conditions and to implement ways to help.

Adding to the hardship, Mama's mother, Francis Grant (known as Pepsi, who must have been experiencing the same conditions in Santa Domingo), stopped sending money to Sophie to help support her daughter. She was also angry that Mama's older sister, Ruth, was pregnant.

Compared to past times when Mama had been well fed, there was very little food in the house then. Mama was unable to quell her dissatisfaction with the scarcity or with food that lacked flavor or which was short of "meat kind."

But the fervent love continued between the two. At fifteen, Mama still slept in the same bed with Sophie. She awoke one morning and noticed that Sophie's feet resembled two overgrown cassava. The doctor was called to the house, as home visits were customary then. His bedside manners were not the most sensitive with poor black people, Mama recalled. He examined Sophie and then, with an indifferent undertone, asked his patient, "You want to go to Fiennes?"

Sophie barely recognized the name "Fiennes" because the term used by ordinary folks like her to indicate the home for the aged was "poor house." People were sent to The Fiennes Institute if their family abandoned them, or "if you had ungrateful children who were dropped in infancy and lost the care of their brain," someone once said.

According to Mama, "...you go dey when you have no body to hand little water give you, and my grandmother wasn't 'de only tree in Gunthrope's pasture. She had me to take care of her. De damn forward and turn-up-nose white doctor."

Sophie looked up at the doctor in confusion. She asked, "Dactor, way name so?"

According to Mama, he replied, with his eyes cold as Ice House, "Poor House!" He knew the local term would drive his message home.

Sophie cried slowly from the bottom of her gut, "Dactor, P-o-o-o-o-r H-o- u - s- e?" She knew she was not destitute. One son was working on and off as a stevedore at the harbor, the other two, though unemployed, were somewhere idling in Gray's Farm. Sophie knew she had good neighbours too, and folks took care of each other back then; families were too proud to relinquish old parents to some institution. His suggestion must have sent shock waves to Sophie's already weak heart.

The young Mama May quickly ran to St. John's, the nearest town, and waited in the doctor's apothecary as he mixed medicine for her grandmother. By the time she left, her cousin, Essie, was hustling up Market Street to find her. When she did so, she looked at her and delivered the news.

"Cousin Miss May, come!" she cried. "Grandie Sophie dead! Grandie Sophie just, dead!" Mama May's world changed from that very moment. She bawled all the way from Market Street to Gray's Farm Road, even more so when someone stopped to inquire, "Little gal for Sophie Daniel, wha mek you ah cry so? Somebody fu you dead?"

Yes, Sophie had ended her reign in Mama's life. It was a hard blow for the granddaughter she had loved, nurtured and pampered over the years. Sophie had kept Mama on a pedestal in the face of challenging and difficult times. She had showed her tremendous love, and kindness, and ingrained a strong sense of pride and dignity.

Sophie had survived through the most difficult times in Antigua outside of slavery. She had transitioned from estate living, where the houses of workers were made of wattle-and-daub—sticks and wood plastered with mud; the bare ground served as the floor. She had toiled tirelessly, picking cotton on estates, or cutting cane on sugar cane plantations, for meager wages. Yet, she had purchased land, and mothered and loved Miss May, consciously teaching her to value herself and to demand respect. That legacy of perseverance, dignity, kindness, and love for others were to become the principles by which Mama would live her life.

At fifteen years old, Mama was about to begin a new phase of her life. She would join the labor force, start her own family and pass the discipline and moral values she had acquired to a future generation. At fifteen, her world would be defined by her own strength to survive and by what she had learned from Sophie's journey.

Pepsi did not return to console her young daughter. She was not willing to leave Santo Domingo for worse hardship in Antigua, so Mama charged ahead like a good racehorse. Sophie had already laid out the blueprint of Mama's path. Another journey was about to begin—one of self-sufficiency, self-dependency, and a readiness to nurture generations of children. Her dream of becoming a teacher was now secondary to her own survival.

CHAPTER THREE

The Mother, Pepsi

"Marry to be a decent young woman"

P EPSI HAD GONE away from Mama for twenty-six years. However, Sophie had taught Mama to honour and respect her mother, even in her absence.

In 1924, Pepsi had traveled to Santo Domingo (now called the Dominican Republic) to care for her sick father. Pepsi left her daughter, Ruth, with her sister, Mam Gigi, and four-year-old Mama with Sophie.

Over the years, Pepsi sent occasional letters with money. All were addressed to Sophie Daniel, never to her young daughter. However, Mama wrote to Pepsi regularly about her progress in school, her dreams of becoming a teacher, and the love and affection she was getting from her grandmother.

At ten, Mama wrote to inform her mother that Sophie had registered her to become an Anglican and that she would be confirmed in a year's time at the St. John's Anglican Cathedral or "Big Church," as it was called. This structure, like the Parthenon in Greece, stood majestically on a rising plot of land in the city of St. John's.

Pepsi wrote back quickly, disappointed with such a decision. Pepsi's argument was based on history: her own grandmother had been born into slavery and had planted many stories in Pepsi's head about life on the plantations. Pepsi's mother had told her about "Big Church" and also about class and race even after slavery. In Pepsi's younger years, it was still the church for whites only, people who could pass as white and the emulators of whites in Antigua.

As I talked to Mama about this particular letter from Pepsi in 1930, we were able to reconstruct the basic content of her mother's message:

January 1930

Dear May,

I hope this letter reach you with the mighty blessings of God, the savior of all men. I am very unhappy that you are walking for confirmation to become an Anglican. I know Sophie is Anglican but it don't mean you have to be one also. I christen you as a child at Greenbay Moravian Church and you go to school there. Sophie can make you receive there. Why she don't send you to Christian Mission to baptize then, just down the road? Your Grandie Sophie should never let you confirm at that church.

When I was a child, my grandmother that born during slavery, told me the slaves couldn't even look up at the statues when they dropped off massa in the horse and cart for church. Even when I was a young girl, that church was not for poor black people. Poor people used to go to the small Anglican church in Point and the one in Johnson's village. This is 1930 and certain type people have names and cushion on seat. And you can't sit any way you please. Take a look at the hanging on the wall, all white massa names that used to beat our people in that church. The money them give to Big Church come from the backs a negga people. My grandmother say

I shouldn't forget and that is why she make sure she tell me, so now am telling you May.

Mark you, I will not be walking up Big Church steps to enter that place now or in the future. God forgive me, but Lord know I mean it from my heart.

Tell your sister Ruth I hear she looking out. Warn her for me, she must get married to be a decent young lady.

Yours faithfully,
Pepsi

At the end of Mama's recollection, I wanted to shout a big hooray to Pepsi, but I did not know how Mama felt about Pepsi's ideas, so I remained silent. I wanted to reassure Mama. I reminded her that I was an Anglican too and that for all the years I had been to this same cathedral, I had loved the church and never for a minute questioned its doctrine or its power to guide me closer to God. However, in my heart, I knew that her mother's letter revealed important history. Pepsi's grandmother had been a slave and her mother had been born less than two decades after the slaves were emancipated.

When I walked for confirmation and attended church services from 1963, I noticed the cushions in the front pews. I watched with curiosity as the fair skinned women, in feathered hats, gloves, and colourful fans, and the men, tucked in woolen suits and bow ties, sat in those pews every Sunday. It did not matter if they arrived early or late or whether it was Easter, Whit Sunday or Christmas Day, those seats were reserved and no one haphazardly sat in them, even if the church was packed and over flowing with people. I would look down from the balcony where we were herded, guarded by sweet smiling nuns, and often wondered why people had to be separated even in church.

I read the hangings on the church walls too, and never made a connection to slavery, the plantations, and the planter class of that time, or to the racism and prejudices that still existed in Antigua.

Although I studied West Indian History in Secondary School, teachers failed to connect what was written in the textbooks to what was happening around us.

I wanted to say another hoorah to Pepsi's ancestors who insisted that such stories be told, and to Pepsi who passed them on to Mama; but I kept my thoughts to myself because Sophie had raised Mama as an Anglican. Mama also raised me as an Anglican. Times changed: Sophie and Mama chose to embrace that change. Mama became a member of the prestigious Anglican Society, and today, I can sit wherever I please in the Anglican Cathedral.

Mama read the letter to Sophie; Sophie was not happy about its content. Sophie was not going to attend one church and send her granddaughter to another. She insisted Mama be confirmed at the "Big Church." The same church Sophie's parents could not enter, and that was gratifying to Sophie.

Mama said, "My Grandie beam that Saturday morning as de white bishop made de sign ah de cross on ma forehead."

Pepsi finally returned to Antigua in 1950, after the death of her husband. Her two daughters had given her grandchildren. Ruth had Wilfred, Buntin, and Kitty. By then Mama had given birth to Rhonie, Pomroy, Elaine, Jerome, Ira; a sixth child, Barrymore, was to be born in a few months.

On the day of Pepsi's arrival, Mama, swollen with pregnancy, was sitting on the stoop of the house. As a plane passed overhead, another yearning for her mother took over her thoughts.

"Eh, I wish my mother was on that plane," she muttered. It must have been premonition. Two hours later, a station wagon pulled up carrying a tall pretty lady, and a handsome fourteen-year-old boy, Mama's brother, Sam.

Mama said, "Monica, ah never cry so." She held her mother close to her pregnant body. Pepsi showed little emotion. Mama believed the reserve was because she had given birth to children out of wedlock. I was surprised by the sadness in her voice the day she told me this, fifty years later.

Pepsi returned to Gray's Farm village as a taciturn and devout Christian. Soon after, she and a woman named Rosie Shaw started the Church of God of Prophesy, called Step Up. The services were held in a small building upstairs of a rum shop in St. John's.

Pepsi often used her sense of moral authority to remind Mama and Ruth of their unmarried status and how disgraceful it was that Mama stayed with a man that kept her constantly pregnant.

"All your unlawful children wrong in God's sight," Pepsi would say. Needless to say, this was always a point of contention. Pepsi saw that Mama had no interest in marriage, and deemed Mama's attitude to be immoral, a sure ticket for a descent into hell. Over the years, Mama tried often to win her mother's love with devotion and attention, but Pepsi, cloaked in religious piety and long sleeves, was unmoved.

Mama said her mother grieved for her dead husband over the years, doted on her son, Sam, but never softened up to her. She said the twenty-six year absence seemed to have destroyed Pepsi's maternal connection to her daughters.

Fuming with hurt and jealousy one day, Mama said to her mother, "You love Sam more than me and Ruth. We're your children too."

Pepsi stared straight into Mama's eyes and replied, "Ah right. He unfortunate, he don't have a father."

In 2007, Sam shed some light on Pepsi's relationship with Mama. He said he had no knowledge before he was fourteen years old that his sisters May and Ruth existed. Sam learned of his sisters in 1950, just a few days before he traveled with his mother to Antigua. Pepsi had never told her husband either that she had two girls back in Antigua. Now I wonder about the many letters Mama wrote during those twenty-six years and the efforts her mother must have employed in order to keep her daughters a secret. Did she not celebrate Mama's achievements in those letters? How could Pepsi not mention Mama's name to her husband for all those years? What could be a mother's reason to deny the existence of her children?

I still have fond memories of Pepsi, and Mama's aunt, Mam Gigi, who lived together across the street from Mama. Mam Gigi had three children. Mam Gigi was a petite, spider-like woman with a flourishing bird's nest of pure white hair. She had lost her sight at an early age, yet her fingers had the aim of an Olympic marksman and her ears, like antenna, worked around the clock. If you gave back talk to her, Mam Gigi's claws zoomed in your direction, grabbing hands full of clothes. If she perceived an inch of disrespect, even directed at someone else, her hearing became alert, and with lightning speed, her claws would clutch layers of clothes down to underwear. We devised ways to unleash ourselves by shedding layers, leaving in her grasp a shirt or sometimes a pair of pants. Once she became privy to our technique, pounds of flesh and clothes filled her claws.

Their house was the largest one on the block. It was tradition then to find, sometimes, up to three generations living under the same roof: their house seemed to contain as many beds as a hospital ward. They held prayer gatherings in their wallpapered living room, which was filled with mahogany furniture, lace doilies and plastic flowers.

Pepsi often peppered her English with Spanish words. Occasionally, when Mama's father, Grandpa Cubana visited, he was the temptation to Pepsi's soul. He would lavish his old "girl friend" with kisses, mostly as a tease to appease onlookers. Pepsi would ignore him, saying that he was drunk and she would condemn his soul to the pits of hell. "Aye, caramba! You bruscapleitos. Brother, you're drunk! Vamanos, you cursed man." His reply was often a mixture of Spanish and English.

"Christ is me rightful judge, hagjow la boca!" was way of telling her to shut up. A spectacle usually ensued as both rained their sparse and broken Spanish on the other.

Children referred to Pepsi as Granny. She was a huge, robust woman who sat as if she were on a throne—shoulders upright, back straight and chin raised. She was never without a pair of stockings rolled in a knot below the knee.

Pepsi had a hearty appetite; it was the cause of frequent belching. In church, she was, of course, most restrained: with a hand across her voluptuous front she would gracefully lift her head upwards, allowing the gas to escape with a quiet "shhhhhhhh" sound that barely parted her lips. At home, however, her belch could be heard from across the street. It thundered after a few slaps between her breasts, roared its way upwards through a wide open mouth packed with dentures, and into a long, loud "doooooooooaaaah!" Everyone thought the sounds were intentional and someone even categorized it as a part of the church lady's suppressed vagabond ways.

Mama's love for her mother was unconditional, though she knew her lifestyle created a permanent rift between them. She was unflinching in her duty to her mother; it was not predicated on reciprocity. Mama always said children should take care of their parents in old age. Sophie had this expectation as well.

When I marvel at Mama's continued commitment even in the absence of love, I realize it came from the teachings of her grandmother Sophie, and the Bible's instruction to honor thy father and mother.

Many years later, when sickness came to Pepsi, it was Mama May who tended to her needs and juggled the two households. Pepsi died in her late seventies and Mama was there to wash the body and prepare it for burial.

CHAPTER FOUR

Uncle Brother - The Father

"Ah Not Going To Hell For This."

MAMA WAS BLESSED with patience. Her father, whom she called Uncle Brother, played her like a skilled obeah man with a voodoo doll. He knew well where to place the pins to elicit the desired response; his character fed on it. As a child, I could not understand why she continued to care for this man that I called Grandpa, except for the fact that he lived too close to our fence to be avoided.

Fences had the same general purpose across the island. Fences were not there merely to indicate land boundaries; they also kept neighbours' eyes out of one another's business. Mama lived on the same parcel of land with her father. A fence split the yard in two, separating both houses. This was not a fence made with straight planks of wood as for a horse's track; it wasn't of mesh wire, nor was it made with pickets of wood to encourage communication. It was made solid, with pieces of old, corrugated, galvanized sheets and scrap wood. Both parties participated in its construction, sealing every nook and cranny, and they kept up the repairs by blocking every hole that appeared.

But nothing could keep Grandpa out of the happenings on Mama's side. His ears never missed the verbal chastisement we received from Mama, or our pleas and cries of pain as Daddy Edmund whipped us. Grandpa would sometimes prance around from a distance, egging on the chastiser. These were his moments of euphoric bliss. He would cackle from his side of the fence, step around in a circle as if he were doing a victory dance, chanting, "Hit dem in dey ear mek dem hear; hit dem in dem head mek dem dead," with every landing of the belt on our backs or bottoms.

As children, we never knew whether or not he was serious about these declarations. Some believed that such cruelty meant he might have been tortured in Cuba during the revolution but no one could confirm that he had been a witness to those events.

Grandpa went to Cuba in the early 1920s during the times when people from the smaller islands went there to work in the sugar industry. When Grandpa left, his daughter was barely a toddler. He returned when she was twelve. In those days children shared beds with parents and so Mama slept in the center, her father and grandmother on either side.

The bond between father and daughter flourished, but it changed after Mama began having children. He, too, was disappointed with the relationship Mama had with Daddy Edmund. Perhaps once Mama decided that she was woman enough to make her own decisions, she ignored Grandpa. The relationship between the two became strained, and Grandpa, annoyed that he could not convince her to leave Daddy Edmund, became disheartened. Given the hardships at the time, and perhaps due to other personal problems, he hid for years behind pints of Cockspur and other rums.

Years later, he, too, became Mama's responsibility, so she washed and cooked for him. However, the images of Grandpa cooking his own meals in his younger days were quite a spectacle. Huge flames wiggled in all directions, out of proportion to the sooty pot. In those days it was not uncommon to create the fire for cooking on the ground between two pieces of steel planks. Pieces of discarded wood and dried twigs provided the fuel. I used to watch the smoke snake its way high up in the air and spread across to our side, causing all eyes in its path to water. Yet Grandpa would sit over this monstrous blob of smoke and flame, an eye squinted against the fumes, a tattered flop hat tilted on the side of his head, sucking on a homemade wooden pipe.

I was mesmerized by the complexity of his appearance, as well. He and Mama shared some resemblance: the same skin tone, equally round faces and pointed noses with slightly flaring nostrils. The similarities ended there. His eyes were an unusual light grey, marbled and strangely soft. Sometimes he appeared as if he were a cornered animal, his sensors tuned to the happenings across the fence; other times, intoxicated with cheap white rum, his grey eyes raged red, like a fire out of control. When he ate, his cheeks moved loosely like doors with broken hinges and his long lips spread low with patches of pink and wetness. Since he was missing most of his teeth, the sides of his face were sunken, giving him a flat yet pugnacious look.

Though we feared him as children, it did not deter us from savoring a giggle behind his back, or doing an occasional mimic of his drunken walk or chants of broken Spanish. We dared him, at times, to chase us. We would step into his yard, in full view, wait until he saw us, and then scramble back to the safety of Mama's house while a thunder of curses pelted our backs. Mama was the one who got blamed.

"May, warn you pickney dem from me!" he would shout. And for minutes after, he would lambaste her, telling her we weren't under "no vine or fig tree," meaning that she allowed us to run wild with no parental guidance, and that inevitably we would "...bite off she ear, as Christ is me rightful judge." Oh how I hated that phrase! The words were hurtful—how could I ever be ungrateful to Mama?

Grandpa was in a world of his own. He had a warped and chauvinistic perception of himself as "a big man."

"I'm a damn big man," he would say. He never used please or thank you for he was "a big man" and a "big man" should never be reduced to such displays of gratitude. Such displays threatened his manhood.

Out of the blue, one day Mama asked him to say please before she handed him dinner.

"Damn forward woman! A damn big man nah say please," he replied as he stormed off to his side of the yard without his dinner. She decided to wait him out. Grandpa was going to say please tonight! He quarreled for what seemed like hours. How long is he going to sit at the entrance of his door without food, I wondered. We all ate dinner, washed dishes— no please from Grandpa. Mama sat down at the back door to her house, darning a pair of pants. He, too, sat at his backdoor cleaning a pair of tall, rubber black boots. An hour passed, and then another. The night was settling over both houses. Mama was showing the patience of Job.

I thought Grandpa might finally be learning a lesson, until Mama's voice penetrated the tense moment.

"Take Uncle Brother food before gas fill he stomach. Ah not going to hell for this," she said to me. "De bible say, honor thy father and mother."

Mama's cousin Chrissie used to say, "Jumbie know who to frighten." Sometimes Grandpa showed softness to others, but Mama was his absolute focus for acrimony. He never gave her eggs from the fowls he raised. Neighbours received such privileges. He never gave the provisions directly to his daughter. He handed us the ground provisions from the land he farmed at Briggins, an area on the outskirts of the city. Everyone said she was often too gentle with him, ignoring the many times when he expressed displeasure with her cooking or the way she parented us. He went to great lengths to antagonize her; but for Mama, this man was her father and deserved respect and love, unconditionally.

One day it was my turn to take dinner over to him. I greeted him.

"Afternoon, Grandpa. Mama send the dinner." He was seated at the back door with a floppy tattered cap on his grey, balding head. His worn clothes were soiled; this was another source of conflict between Mama and him.

Once I overheard Mama saying, "Uncle Brother, anybody see you so dirty would think you have nobody to look after you." He cackled then, an impish light dancing in his eyes, amused by the thought of someone degrading his daughter.

He said, "Dat is what ah want them to say. Woman, ah change when ah feel, I'm a damn big man."

In my hands were fungee and stewed fish, his favorite meal. Not expecting a thank you, I put the bowl in his hand, and then hustled across the yard. Seconds later, the dinner took flight: gliding over the six-foot fence were the ball of fungee, the sauce, and the stew followed by the sound of the enamel bowl clanking on the stone heap in the yard.

"Wha blasted small ball ah fungee dat?" he shouted out to Mama. "Damn big man me be!" Mama May never said a word. The next day, of course, there was my cousin Fitzroy or me with Grandpa's meal.

For many years I listened to Grandpa's constant displeasure with Mama's cooking: the rice grains were hard enough to "knock dong bird," the fish too small, "just suit pickney," and "de food fresh and warnt more salt." Grandpa never got the full "length of a rope," which was Mama's indication that she had had enough. Why did she tolerate this type of treatment? How could she withstand his constant barrage and not defend herself? Sometimes I wondered if he had broken her and she had resigned herself to silence where he was concerned. Grandpa, aside, she was aggressive with her family, defensive against unfair treatment of neighbours, and extremely opinionated about the politics of the island. I could not understand her unshakeable sense of loyalty to him.

Sitting at the end of our fence was a date tree. Although the roots were mainly in our section of the yard, the lush, juicy, abundance of dates fell on to Grandpa's side. We had complete autonomy to ravage our side of the date tree, but on Grandpa's side it was like the fox trying to reach the grapes. The plump sweet fruits would ripen for days, only to rot on the ground. We hoped that any hidden softness in this, thin cantankerous man would surface.

We would ask, "Grandpa, can we pick dates?" Often the answer was no.

"No badder me head, you pickney dem fu May. You all too damn lick'rish." That was another word I hated with venom, "lick'rish." We weren't greedy or deprived. All we wanted were dates; we were family, his grandchildren. We bought his cigarettes from the shops, purchased pints of rum for him without Mama knowing, and dropped off sweet potatoes he sent to neighbours. Occasionally, overcome by daring, we would attack the tree, scrambling on the ground for the fruits then quickly running to the safety of Mama's yard under a hail of curses and threats. It was another occasion for Grandpa to attack his daughter.

"May, warn you pickney an' dem from me. Tell dem not to come in me yard or ah bus dem head, as Christ is me rightful judge. You over-love dem with ignorance. You have dem under no vine or fig tree, you hear me!"

Mama would respond, "They're you grandchildren. You give strangers the dates, but not them. Who help look after you when you sick, strangers? Who run you errands, strangers?"

"Well, don't send dem to do nothing for me," he would reply. "Let me die in yah, as Christ is my rightful judge." He would continue to fuss alone, for Mama realized that that was the way he was and no one was going to change him. Sometimes, at the end of the quarrel, he would walk towards the date tree with a stick, knock hundreds of the ripe fruits to the ground, and then bark at us, "You pickney Dem for May. Come pick up de dates." As we happily pushed one another, collecting bowls of the fruit, he would hustle back to his house and close the door. At the time, I thought that he did not want to see the pleasure he had given. It was several years later that I realized the opposite was true. He did not want us to see the pleasure we gave him.

Somewhere buried inside that bony exterior was love. It surfaced unrestrained when he saw vulnerable babies crawling, or toddlers running around. At one moment he would curse every living thing;

the next moment he would grab the youngest grandchild, smother it with kisses, and smack its delicate jaws with his sloppy, toothless mouth while the child struggled for freedom.

"Grandpa love you," he would say, making playful noises with his lips as he nudged his grey-bearded chin under the babies' ribs, tickling these innocents into a frenzy of laughter. The "love episode" often ended with Mama's intervention, rescuing them from his grasp.

"Uncle Brother, don't pawn de child face with your rum mouth!" she scolded. The baby's plump cheeks now glistened with Grandpa's saliva and sweat.

"Woman, you damn forward, tha's me gran'chile. Who best to kiss dem?" Grandpa would laugh, displaying his pink gum and few teeth.

"Keep you germs to you'self," Mama would shoot back at him.

"Damn forward, a blasted big man you talking to!" He would curse as he sauntered off to sit at the entrance of his house, the tattered floppy hat flailing in his arm.

The dynamics existing between them seemed volatile from my point of view, but Mama found levity at times. Years after, I asked her why she allowed Grandpa to curse and attack her.

"I love my father, you know. I love him very much."

"Even after he cursed you, Mama?" I asked.

"Yes. After a while it didn't bother me because I tried to understand him. Uncle Brother was sick. I believe as he got older he hide behind the bottle." The love was evident in her eyes. Grandpa Cubana had difficulty readjusting to Antigua when he returned from Cuba: he spent time in the psychiatric hospital on his return. Perhaps he harbored some guilt over leaving Mama as a small child, with a mother who also left.

I wasn't ready to rationalize his behaviour as quickly.

Sick? Excuses, excuses, I thought. "He was always chasing us like wild cattle, Mama!" I said aloud.

"He didn't mean half the things he say, chile. It just made him feel like a big man." We laughed together at her last two words. How often had they bounced on our eardrums?

I cannot recall a peaceful conversation between them and it got worse indeed as Grandpa aged. When there was a show of genuine concern on her part, he responded explosively with a show of his maleness, his 'big man' status. But though I watched Mama struggle at times to be calm and devoted, very rarely did she lose patience; her many threats to stop cooking for him never came to fruition.

Her mantra was "Uncle Brother, you lucky you' my father." She remained like the Rock of Gibraltar, unshaken by his eccentric ways. I often wished that she would relinquish that responsibility at times, but her commitment was steadfast. After all, did she not care for me and a house full of children with the same unwavering attitude?

Years before he died, at the age of eighty-four, he quit the bottle cold turkey, and lost the fire for conflict. It was not the result of any outside intervention, no threat from Mama, just the actions of "a big man."

One night, as she wiped him down from a high fever, she said he wished he would die. Mama concluded that he was in dire pain, but he never complained. Perhaps, due in part to his notions of being "a damn big man."

Mama suspected that he had prostate cancer, due to his enlarged scrotum. She moved him into one of the bedrooms in her house and cared for him with her usual devotion. The morning of the day he died, she made breakfast for him.

"Uncle Brother," she called. A strange quietness lingered in the room; his body barely created a bulge on the iron cot that morning. "Ah going to work, remember to eat yuh breakfast."

His reply was feeble, but she heard clearly. "The Lord be wid you till you come," he answered. It was a tenderness Mama had not heard from him since she was young.

Later that day, a telephone message from the local police station told her to come home from work immediately. It was a grandchild who discovered Grandpa dead, one hand hanging off the side of the bed, a few inches within reach of his breakfast.

Mama tore a piece off the bed sheet, tied his big toes together, and rested his hands across the chest. She cried, the sound lifting from way inside her gut. Emotions of love, silently suppressed for years, were freed from the cavern of her soul. I wonder what her thoughts were as she cried for him. Did she reflect on her grandmother Sophie who had, after all, given her Grandpa? Did her body shake from the memories of precious times between father and child, or was it from memories of the years of conflict and unexpressed love? I couldn't understand the feelings of losing a parent because my own parents had passed away before my comprehension of death. But I felt saddened by Mama's grief.

I have a new fondness for Grandpa these days. I am able to reflect on the times he was unkind with a new understanding, and even laughter. Now as adults, Mama's children can look back and admire her stamina, and remember how her respect and love for Grandpa were unending. Of course she demanded that we show him respect, but she also demonstrated what devotion to a parent meant. To this day, when there is a family gathering, Grandpa's weird habits are always a topic of discussion, for we are now able to find levity in the memories of his character.

CHAPTER FIVE

Mama At My Father's Funeral

"...Don't Worry Chile ..."

OR ALL MY years growing up, my father continued to live in my head, though he had been dead since 1959. His memories were not kept alive by any sweetness, warmth, or even love, for I had never learned that I should love him. It was the taunting of childish rivalry that resurrected my father every time and caused a blanket of sadness to come over me.

"Go look for your own dead Pupa," or "you father done dead and bury," the other children taunted.

Tears.

Adults bent on molding good character in me, often referred to my status as an orphan. "Child, you fatherless and motherless, behave you self."

Tears.

I was blamed for my parents' deaths in moments of puerile stubbornness.

"Chile, you too stubborn, you nah go kill me off like you Muma and Pupa."

Tears, tears, tears.

At the public standpipe when I fought for and victoriously regained my turn to fill a bucket with water, a strange taunt about my father's death spewed from the mouths of young fallen rivals.

"Ah good yuh father dead!"

As an introduction to someone unfamiliar with my lineage, Mama explained, "... dis is de chile Ruth and Daniel dead lef. Is Edmund's dead brother daughter."

As a child, simply eating a piece of candy could trigger a genuine memory of my father. It is my earliest memory. My father stands over me with hands extended. He is offering me something to eat from pockets bulging with local confectionaries—sugar babies, peppermint sticks, sugar cakes, cake tarts or butter flaps. I have his total attention, so I return his show of affection with hugs and kisses. Mama is close by. She smiles because I giggle while strands of sweet saliva escape my lips, running down my chin to the white collar of a yellow flowered frock. I am between two and four years old.

Often another memory follows, one with much more detail. I am at a family gathering. Mama is always part of the picture, and her voice is like custard porridge—smooth, sweet, and warm. Later, I am cuddled in bed while a world of imagined fears lurks around and the man is there again with candy just for me.

My father's face had been permanently etched in my mind. His smooth dark skin shone like new pennies on his tall slouching body; he had an almost perfect set of teeth, white like rice porridge, and a smile like you would see on a Colgate commercial. A fusion of Old Spice cologne and a pleasant grassy sourness inhabited his hairy neck. His eyes were most memorable for they danced in deep shadowed sockets when he played with me, and later gazed sadly when he spoke to his brother, Daddy Edmund, and Mama. His eyes became sad when the conversation drifted to his lost wife, my mother Ruth, and my brothers and sisters, who had been dispersed like petals from the stamen of a hibiscus after her death.

With maturity and Mama's help, I was able to piece his story together. My father, a man who desired to care for his own family, had failed. His wife, my mother, died after childbirth, and left him alone to care for six young children. The family slowly began to fall apart. One of his children left to live in another village with my grandmother, Annie Jacob; he cried silently. As Mama and Daddy Edmund walked away with me—a child he had ably kissed and hugged, fed, and giggled with—he was broken. When my newborn sister Avril died soon after, and the others left in his care could not be cared for well enough, he lost confidence. My father was crushed. He was no longer a man. The losses were too much and too soon, one after another. Eventually, he died too.

As I grew older, snippets of my father jumbled and flashed in and out of my consciousness—at play, at school, at church, at night, and during fights as I defended my father's memory against verbal barbs.

I was only four years old when he passed. Perhaps childhood fantasy and relentless teasing over the years affected the details of my father's funeral in my mind. In any case, the day and its aftermath left a lasting imprint on my psyche.

The day of the gathering for the funeral could have started like any ordinary day growing up on Gray's Farm Road. The roosters, nature's timekeepers, would perch on galvanized fences or wooden fowl coops and crow chaotically at dawn. I would awake, hearing the distant braying of a donkey, barking dogs, chickens clucking and pecking at corn, and the grunts of Mama May's pigs awaiting their first meal. Fever grass tea would be simmering on a coal pot nearby.

On that particular morning, as I ate cornmeal porridge and drank the fever grass tea, the sight of a tub of water bothered me. It was still but threatening, in the early glare of mid-morning sun. As a small child, the bath pan was a nemesis —it signaled either a bath or a hair washing. I detested both, but every sinew in my body dreaded the latter. There was a laundry list of reasons to dislike washing my hair: the shampoo burned my eyes, the conditioner smelled like foul eggs, the water was either too hot or too cold, but most important of all, I nearly drowned every time.

Up until the age of twelve, washing my hair was symbolically a Roman contest: the yard was the Coliseum, my cousins and Grandpa, the spectators, and in the center, I was the little gladiator, filled with venom yet deeply afraid. I was the lamb to be slaughtered, mimicked and laughed at, even days after. I hated the jeers. I hated the tub. I hated my opponent, who head-locked me under a sweaty armpit for eternity while fingers tugged roughly at my coarse, short hair. Every pound of my body struggled vehemently against brawn and what felt like an oil drum of water pouring over my head. My thin legs kicked in all directions. I heaved like a wild horse to surface, and, though bridled by someone's heavy hands, I pushed up with all my might to suck in a gulp of air. They did not understand the fear; they did not know how stifling, how suffocating it felt. The water flooded my nose and something in my chest seemed about to burst. They didn't know I was drowning, and no one took me seriously when I tried to explain.

Then, as if on cue, Grandpa would extend his hands—just like Caesar—saying, "Hold her down tight." It was the last stab.

At nine o'clock that morning I was given the death sentence: my hair would be washed. I trembled once again from fear. Minutes later, I was clenched under my Cousin Elaine's armpits—an instant enemy— as torrents of water tumbled over my head. I started to suffocate, but Mama came to the rescue, my savior once again.

"Mercy, be gentle," she said. "You know de child don't like water pour over her head. Turn her back way Elaine." Mama pulled me away from Elaine's grasp, the soapsuds running down my chest. "Wash de girl hair back way, nobody care dat she 'fraid the water over her face. Have some pity Lord!"

Cousin Elaine laughed and concluded that I was "just nasty."

Grandpa commanded, "Hold her down tight ah say." Mama ignored the jeers and for the hundredth time demonstrated how it should be done. It was always Mama and me against the rest of the yard.

By afternoon, the house buzzed with voices, and filled with the smells of johnnycakes and salted fish.

"Where me handkerchief?"

"Anybody see the shoe whitening?"

I asked, "Way we going?" No one answered. All my cousins were dressed in black, white, purple or dark blue. Mama dressed me in a beautiful, new white frock. I knew something special was happening because new dresses were ordinarily for weddings or important church days like Harvest, Easter, and Confirmation.

"I go to church Mama?" I asked as she braided my hair and tied two white ribbons on the side braids.

"No, me chile." She retied a huge sash in the back of the dress. A slight smile curled her lips, her stumpy fingers tugging at the hem to even the edges.

"I going to 'real' school then." I was still attending a nursery in St. John's.

"No Monica, not church, not school.....eh, eh.......we going to see family. Your own people," she explained. She then patted my bottom, crushing the layers of satin and lace. There my questions ended, for her touch was like a johnnycake—sweet and comforting. "Don't worry chile, Mama here for you. Look how pretty Mama girl look."

This dress was different. It was white. Mama knew my favorite colours were yellow and pink, but this dress was pretty nonetheless. A row of lace rounded the neck. It had a pocket on each side, a skirt that flared, and small pearl buttons running down the center. Someone had whitened an old pair of patent leather shoes, and given me socks. I was happy, pretty, and anxious to go. Even Grandpa, who never dressed up, sported a rumpled black suit, the only one he owned. Looking across the yard he declared for the hundredth time how vain I was and that "May, you treat she like a show-piece, always dressing she up." If he were not going with us, he would have sauntered off a few yards to sit in the shade of a date tree to continue the fuss.

The neighbourhood cab driver Mama had hired, arrived. Surely, this must be a special event, I surmised. Daddy Edmund and his other children had gone ahead in a bus. "The chile will come with me," Mama told him. Two other people climbed into the car with me.

On this day, the ride to the country was not much different from the many trips with Daddy Edmund or Mama that I would take in the future. The smell of flowers and herbs perfumed the countryside; gardens of crotons, poinsettias, hibiscus, huge tamarind trees and lampposts skipped backwards as we drove. At the side of the road, children made faces as they stood and waited when we interrupted a cricket match. My head darted every which way, my eyes following the women carrying heavy loads on their heads. When I closed my eyes, the fresh breeze caressed my face as Mama's strong grip restrained me in my seat. Like any children on a long trip, I asked the inevitable question: "Mama, we there yet?"

"Chile, we're in the country now, in St. Phillips." I followed a large drop of sweat on her forehead and watched it fall towards her cheek. She raised a jolly arm, thick as a slab of ham, and, with a huge handkerchief, mopped the life out of it. In those days she was like the Aunt Jemima lady on a box of pancake mix, with plump cheeks, and eyes that closed to savor a laugh that shook her high belly.

As the ride continued, her eyes were red and distant and her shoulders drooped. Pouting her pair of thin lips, she seemed in deep thought. The curls pressed into her hair had slowly lost shape with the sun's heat. They now dangled, burdened by sweat and the playfulness of the island breeze. I climbed into her lap and another ball of sweat skated down a cheek.

"Mama, you crying?" I asked.

"No, me dear chile, is just sweat from the broiling sun." She let out a sigh and gave me 'the eye'—a signal to end the questioning. From an early age, children learn when to cease asking questions. There were subtle ways to shut us up: adults widened their eyes, shifted them way into the corner of sockets, clamped their lips like pliers, or jutted their jawbones. Mama May was crying, but I was too tired, and too sleepy, to find out why.

After what seemed a long time, we drove onto a narrow street covered with white pebbles. We stopped at a small white cement house with a patch of flowers in the front. I had never seen so many people clustered in a street before. I wanted to run to the people I recognized: my sisters, Eunette and Yvonne, my brothers, Dunstan and Eardley, my Cousin Inez, my Uncle John, and many others. Mama was right; I was truly going to see family. Everybody wanted to touch me. Mama seemed to beam with pride as she held onto my hand.

"Chile, stay with Mama," she said. Then, for a moment, her hand loosened as Pomroy, one of her sons, extended his. Immediately, he scooped me into his arms. As he hugged me, a sudden, strange sound startled me; it was a wail that thundered from the bottom of Pomroy's belly. The sound shook his chest and contorted his face, squeezing a long trail of tears down his sweaty, dark cheeks. This was my first memory of seeing a male in tears. I would hear a similar sound from Mama almost sixteen years later when she received news of the death of her oldest daughter, Rhonie. I felt sad for Uncle Pomroy then and may have started to curl my lips to cry, but he rested me on his shoulders. Then I saw it. I saw everything from his shoulders, because there was a gap in the crowd. How long did I stay on his shoulders? Perhaps not long, in actual time, but long enough to see and remember I had seen this man before. It was long enough to recall the sweetness of his pockets. It was long enough to thirst again for his candy treats. That was all I knew and could think about: the man who had always given me candy was lying in a box.

As if with a camera, I snapped his face and his picture snuggled and settled in my head, where it remains to this day. His face was ashy, his eyes more sunken than usual, and his lips unfriendly. My father's cheeks looked as if he had been sucking on lollipops but had forgotten to relax his jaw. I was passed from one family member to the next and finally back to Mama May. She used her perfumed handkerchief to wipe my forehead while her own face drowned in sweat.

Slowly, the adults moved onto the main street in two lines, stopping before a yard filled with plants, flowers, and huge square stones. Everyone looked solemn and pitiful.

"Hold onto my dress, chile. You stay with Mama," Mama directed. She seemed guarded and restrained. She sang but not in the cadence that usually lulled me to sleep as she combed my hair or sat over a tub washing clothes in her yard. I saw her tears and wondered if Mama was crying for me, but I still could not understand why. I was dressed up, everyone said I was pretty, and Uncle Pomroy had even given me a shoulder ride. Why was Mama still sad?

I wanted to distance myself for a while. Why was the candy man taking so long to extend his hands? I needed to find him, but to do that I would have to leave Mama's side. My chance came when Aunt Grace came over to talk. I let go of Mama's dress and ploughed my way through the shrubs in the yard, moving closer to a man with a book. He giggled and smiled down at me. I grabbed his long white gown and edged my way close to his legs, flanked by the hem of his long clothing. I wanted to see what was drawing everyone's attention. After slipping in the dirt, I quickly dusted my hands on my dress. There was the wooden box again, with varnish like Mama's floor painted for Christmas. A fat rope guided by two men in tall rubber boots supported the box, while two rusted shovels stood in a heap of fresh bronze soil. I wanted to see where the box was going; I tried to follow its movement while the sad singing became louder. Just when I was about to leap forward, dreamlike, thirsting for candy, I felt hands, tugging and tugging at me, pulling me away, lifting me in a tight hug close to a bosom with a familiar smell. It was Mama; my face was now cushioned against her wide body.

Tears skated down her cheeks once again and, as she fussed about my soiled dress, someone said, "Nah worry, she carn't remember notten Miss May." That was all I heard, and that was all I remembered. Mama fussed about the dress, while I wondered about the man and my candy. The dull sounds of a song faded behind our backs. In my childish state, I believed that the man could not rest for too long inside the box amidst the terrible singing.

After the funeral, we headed back to Gray's Farm with a new addition to Mama's household: my brother Eardley. Dunstan and Yvonne permanently joined Grandmother Annie in Parham. The white cement house with the small flower garden was left empty. A silence followed us home to Gray's Farm like a hungry stray cat; each of us buried in our own feelings of fatigue, fear, sadness, and loss

Drifting off to sleep later that night, I heard the sounds of cousins whispering. I watched fearfully as shadows formed from clothes hanging on the partition around the room. The shapes were of animals and what seemed like a slouching man extending his arms to me, but it changed as the night's breeze licked the flame from the oil-burning lamp on the dresser. A sweet smell of rose powder and perspiration suddenly filled my nostrils. I knew that wonderful and familiar smell—Mama. There now was Mama's hand tapping, tapping a rhythmic beat on my back as I snuggled in the bed, the same hands that had rescued me from Elaine's grip in the morning, and had saved me from following the box that afternoon. I felt reassured, though thoughts of the candy man were still in my head: his ashy look in the box, and the sad singing for his ears. Were Mama's tears and Pomroy's wails for him? I wanted to love the candy man like I loved Mama, but I did not know how.

CHAPTER SIX

Mama Is Pregnant

"Babies Come From Heaven, Tek Care of Dem"

WHEN YOU ARE five years old and busy absorbing the world around you, some things just float by unseen, unnoticed— even some things as big as Mama May being pregnant with twins.

I had no information about pregnancy, and as with all children, I wanted to know where babies come from. "Babies come from heaven," I heard Mama say repeatedly. She gave the same answer when her daughter, Rhonie, came home with Dave, Mama's first grandchild. Over the years when Andy, Byron, Andrea, Jeanelle, Mervin, Junior, Shanara and a host of others were born, Mama would tell their parents that they all came from heaven. "Tek care of dem," she advised.

When Josephine, the young next-door neighbour came home with a baby, I asked Mama about babies and gathered this information:

"Josephine went up the hill by the hospital and get a baby, chile."

Mama returned home from the hospital with two babies of her own in 1960.

Amazingly, I have no recollection of Mama's belly before the deliveries. If I can remember my father's funeral, how is it that a twin pregnancy eludes me? Pregnant with my first child, Monifa, many years later, I was large. My stomach was impossible to miss. So Mama with twins must have been inescapable. I try to rationalize that Mama's days of pregnancy may not have been dramatic as mine.

She often boasted that she worked "up to de last day before me water break to deliver nearly all of me children." I paced for three days in Holberton hospital with my first pregnancy, while a ten-pound baby, three weeks over due, refused to be born. Who visited Mama at hospital then, as she did for me, bringing food and taking away nightgowns to be washed? Who rubbed Mama's forehead as she did mine from the high fever I had for days on end?

The moment of her arrival with the babies is clear to me, though. The sun was blazingly hot. It had eaten away at the dark clouds and spread a shadow from the detached kitchen to a portion of the yard, covering the stone heap. Cousin Elaine had fed us some bread and butter and some lemongrass tea with hot cow's milk when news surfaced that Mama was coming home with two babies. Mama had been gone for days, but my inquiries as to her whereabouts had always ended in teasing.

"Cry baby, Mama gone lef you, she nah come back," someone had chimed. I must have cried, for my tears flowed easily in those days. I cried even when songs were sung—another reason for teasing me when I was little.

I can imagine how my feet skipped around the two-bedroom house, perhaps dressed in a floral yellow frock, my short braids uncombed for the whole time Mama had been away. Imagine the commotion: Cousin Elaine rushing around collecting pieces of clothing that had been strewn around the floor during the previous days, Fitzroy, eleven months older than me, zooming paper planes across the room, and me, the little girl, cutting dresses from an old Simplicity catalogue. Daddy Edmund would have left for work at the sugar factory earlier, calling behind a warning that he would scold them for not doing chores. The other children might have gone to school.

About one in the afternoon, Mama, at forty years of age, emerged from Mr. Artwell's station wagon with a human parcel in each arm.

She beamed like a lighthouse, smiling from ear to ear and looking at me.

"Come, secon," she said ('secon' was a colloquial term of endearment). "Mama bring something for you." The babies' eyes were set in tiny heads. Mama looked at me, awaiting a response.

Cousin Fitzroy shoved ahead and, pointing at the larger baby, said, "Dat one for me, Mama." He touched the baby's oversized feet in a clumsy show of affection. The baby raised his clasped hands and wrinkled feet slowly in protest.

"Be careful, Fitzy, dey not playthings. Babies are soft and weak," she warned, tucking the blanket under the baby's feet. Close up, the babies, named Patmore and Barrymore, looked like two of the piglets under the shed from the perpetual litter in our yard. This was Mama's second attempt at naming a son Barrymore: the other child had died in 1950.

To own a child was not a bad thing after all, so I claimed Barrymore as mine. Though only five, I had learned that cooperation was vital to survival in a small space that had become overcrowded. I set to the task of helping Mama with the twins.

Mama used to say, "…sink or swim." So swim I did! As Mama's little apprentice, I fetched powder, towels and so on. I saw how she cooled the milk to perfect temperature, and tested it by squirting it on the back of her hand. She often gave the leftover milk to me. I learned quickly, and she would rub my forehead saying, "You're my little left hand, chile. You are only five but you sorbice. The Lord bless you." Her words and actions inspired me. Mama was teaching me how valuable babies were. She said babies were precious gifts and that these two were lucky to have a big sister. I didn't agree entirely. To me, they were also intruders, slowly taking Mama away from me, filling her arms with their frail bodies—arms that were no longer mine alone to seek comfort.

"Secon, Mama breast hurt right now, you can't lean too hard." I had squeezed my way into her lap.

"Why dey hurt?" I asked. I wasn't happy that the babies were causing her pain, not at all. It was a conflicted time for me—enjoying the babies, yet slowly losing my position with Mama and the women around her.

The women crossed the street to visit the new center of attraction. They brought gifts of fruits, vegetables, cake, cow's milk, and hand-sewn baby clothes. I imagined they must have done the same when I arrived from St. Phillip, each woman taking her part in the raising of every child in the village.

First to arrive was Miss Rosie, with an air of authority and her head held high, like Mama on Easter Sunday. With her head wrapped in red cloth, Miss Rosie whirled gracefully into the house. She walked straight to the bedroom, and the babies screamed in unison as she entered. A window allowed some sunlight into the small bedroom that was overstocked with bundles of clothes. Miss Rosie's dark complexion was a striking contrast to the milky-white hair braids extending to her ears. She was well respected in the community, and had healed many children whose ribs got "out of place" or whose "stomach fall." There were conditions that older folks believed conventional doctors couldn't diagnose or fix. Whenever anyone in the village had a high fever, Miss Rosie would also bathe them with herbs like mulberry, sour sop leaves, cattle tongue, and privy.

Oblivious to my presence, Miss Rosie spat out instructions to Mama. "Miss May, keep dey feet warm. Watch de draught from dem head." She strutted like a chanticleer, withdrew the piece of mosquito netting, examined the babies' feet and palms for any sight of yellowing, then remarked, "Dey look good Miss May, don't 'fraid to feed dem de bottle. Two pickney tough to breast-feed. Draw some marjoram with glucose and don't mek deh suck you dry. Don't badder wid de backra doctor uptown. Lickle bush won't hurt dem. You need plenty rest, too."

She made it clear that Mama was to keep the umbilical area dry and wrapped with a belly band to protect and keep air out of the babies' navels. Mama was further instructed to bring Patmore and Barrymore to Miss Rosie after five days. I learned later that the withered piece that fell off of the navel was usually buried in the yard to confirm one's birthright. The local saying was "my nable 'tring buried yah."

Then Miss Freda arrived. I called her the sugar lady because she made sugar cakes, fudge, and peppermint candy and sold them at the market. Whenever she visited Mama, she usually brought a taste of something for me, but that day she had nothing. She was all excited about the twins and passed me like a stranger as I sat over a bowl of oatmeal porridge.

"Eh, eh, ley me see de little man and dem," she said as she pushed everyone aside with her large body. I always stared at her elbows; they were dimpled with fat.

"Tut...tut..tut. Dey so lickle May, but cute, mind you." She wiped her hands on her apron and lifted up Barry, holding him up high.

That's my baby, I thought, put him down!

"Ah who dis one," she asked Mama. I was still hoping something would spring from her pocket, but Miss Freda drooled over the babies and ignored the fact that I had abandoned my food and was now pulling her skirt, trying to give her the names of the babies. On her next statement, I let go. It was confirmation that these little ones had truly taken my position.

"Wake up," she said, shaking their saggy legs. "Dis Miss Freda, open you eyes man, you soon be eating me sugar cakes and things." I could not believe it — another of my privileges to be shared?

Old folks were invaluable in child rearing. Aunt Toonkoo lived on the land that adjoined us on the left. She was the oldest person I knew. She walked folding over like a leaf with a stick. Thin and frail, we called her "Ant Toonkoo" because she was really scrawny like ants. Her face would be an artist's dream. It was gaunt and indented in the places where muscle and fat had once dwelled. Silvery hair hung in thin braids at the sides of her madras head cloth. She never wore a simple skirt and blouse set or a single garment like a dress; instead she layered all three garments, overlaid with an apron. The edges were frayed, but every piece was always clean, sometimes starched stiff and even ironed. Her thin fingers were like dried twigs with blue blood veins running beneath the skin. She was the local medicine woman and the only person who could command a group of children to drink Epsom salts, a dreadful tasting laxative, at will. Everyone in the village revered her.

Aunt Toonkoo wobbled into the house with her walking stick to perform a ritual; a scent of Canadian healing oil and Iodex followed her closely. Those who were present stepped back as she stood near the twins gesturing the sign of the cross. She opened the Bible Mama had on the dresser, and placed it on the pillow above their heads. She spread a pair of scissors and placed them on the Bible to keep bad spirits away. Then she opened a bottle of rose oil, sprinkled it in the corners of the room and, without uttering a word, departed. I watched from the window, open-mouthed with wonder as she crossed the footpath back to her house and shut the door. Mama looked pleased; the babies were safer now.

Strangely, none of the men came to visit the babies. I couldn't understand it, then. I watched Daddy Edmund put physical distance between himself and the twins: he tried to connect remotely from the entrance of the door as the babies wiggled in the bed. He smiled slightly, watching and listening to the sounds. You knew he was proud, but men did not hold small babies at that time.

Everyone chipped in to care for the twins. On any given day, a neighbour was in the yard assisting with the washing, or someone was sitting under the shade of a tree hushing a baby to sleep, while Mama prepared dinner. However, Mama still stole a moment to comb my hair or to bathe me. In the midst of all this activity, Mama was teaching me how to care for children.

"Babies come from heaven," she would repeat from time to time. Perhaps she was saying that children were God's blessing, and with that belief in mind, she never turned a child away from her door.

I saw, too, the camaraderie that existed between Mama and her neighbours—the respect, kindness and love they had for her. The women were carrying on a tradition that they too had learned from parents before them. They were now instructors, guidance counselors, nurses, doctors, and chastisers in the twin's lives. This was the custom in small villages: every adult was a parent and could give you a spanking without your parents' permission.

Although she seemed exhausted, Mama kept going, day after day, providing for the others in the household. The babies had an endless list of needs and the women of the neighbourhood waited at her beck and call. However, Patmore died a year and half later. I remember thinking at that time; maybe it would be easier for Mama, now that Patmore is back in heaven.

CHAPTER SEVEN

Raising Children

"All Children Need A Wash 'Kin And Little Food"

O NE OF MAMA'S sayings was "…all children need is a good wash 'kin and little food." Though it was her way of trivializing the task of raising children, as a young girl in the house, I could see that raising children was much more intense and difficult. They came in droves to an already crowded house. Some came without food, clothes, and good discipline. Like Andy, who was asthmatic, some came with earaches and nosebleeds, and in the case of baby Patmore—pain for Mama.

"No mother like to lose a chile," she told me.

The number of children that surrounded her never seemed to matter. It started in the early 1960s. Dave, a first grandchild, was left in her care when his mother went abroad. Then Cousin Elaine left her son, Andy. In time, more came, and more stayed: Andrea, Byron, Shanara, Geanelle, Mervin, Junior, Ira's daughter Monica, Sharifa, Cora, Sabira, Chamelle, Tammy, Brent, Barrcia, Peppe, and many more.

Byron's arrival was one of the most memorable. His mother Celeste, who lived in All Saints Village, was despondent over her relationship with Mama's son, Jerome, coupled with the task of taking care of a baby. When Byron was just a few months old, Celeste appeared at Mama's gate, baby in her arms and nothing else for the child: no clothes, no food, and no bottles.

"Miss May, hold de child for me because ah going to the Virgin Island on a short holiday," Celeste said.

"Celeste, why you didn't bring de chile stuff? Mama asked.

"Don't worry Miss May, ah go bring dem tomorrow," she assured Mama.

Well, Byron never got his things. Celeste occasionally visited over the years.

Byron joined his mother in the Virgin Islands when he was fifteen years old. However, Celeste sent him back to Antigua after only a week. Byron barely had enough cab fare to get to Gray's Farm Village from the airport. The cab driver left him at The Bridge, a quarter mile away, and he walked the rest of the way right into Mama's arms, carrying an even smaller suitcase than the one he took to St. Thomas. Influenced by Mama's strong parental guidance, love and insistence on education, Byron grew up to become the second teacher Mama raised and, later, the first lawyer in the family.

By 1967, most of Mama's grown children were living in the Virgin Islands and in New York, and many grandchildren were coming under her care for varying periods of time. Another stage of our relationship began then. As the only young girl in the house, many chores fell into my lap.

When Mama cooked during the week, I passed ingredients to her as she sat stationary around a coal pot. I learned to measure the correct ratio of water to rice, learned how to avoid lumps in the fungee, and learned the names of fish we bought at the market. Here again, Mama was practicing what her grandmother had done with her years before. Once I started to learn Home Economics at the

Princess Margaret School, Sunday dinner became my responsibility completely. Mama enjoyed special dishes I made like shepherd's pie, braised chicken and vegetables au gratin.

By my early teen years, Mama ceased doing the food shopping. It was a chore she had disliked and now that I was old enough to "cut and contrive," now that I could compare prices at different shops, I took over the task.

Though my assistance offered some relief to Mama as far as meals and house cleaning were concerned, the bundles of dirty clothes around the house still overwhelmed her. Sometimes, with the children abroad sending money and clothing, she paid a local washerwoman to assist. I knew Mama was trying to help someone else who had difficulty "cutting and contriving." She knew the person was struggling, and perhaps unemployed; maybe the man in the house was not pulling his weight, or perhaps there was no man in the house at all.

Though she successfully moved like a racehorse between one grandchild and another, I still could not see how raising children could be considered easy.

When the children became sick, home remedies were always the first thing tried. For a fever, Mama mixed a warm carbolic bath to snuff the heat out of the child's body; for colds she gave anything from castor oil to a cup of tea made with cattle tongue leaves. Babies who would not sleep at night drank sour sop or marjoram tea. For asthma, heavy chest colds, or wheezing, Mama wrapped a salve of soft candle and nutmeg on brown paper around the afflicted child's chest. This was believed to be effective so long as the salve was removed before sunrise next morning. She administered horrible-tasting drafts of wormgrass tea or green syrupy medicine from the local chemist to rid our bowels of worms.

Conventional doctors were a last resort because there was little money for private medical attention, and a doctor's visit at the public clinic meant long hours sitting on wooden benches. When such a visit proved necessary, Mama seldom took just one child. Instead, she would scoop up all the young ones together so that those who were not sick got a much-needed check-up or a supply of medicine for later use. We looked forward to such visits because there would be special treats from Mama, like crackers, cheese, soft drink, Shirley Biscuits, and fancy cookies to eat. We stuffed crackers into the soft drink bottles and the fun was to retrieve the soaked pieces, often to no avail.

Since relatives surrounded us for many years along Gray's Farm Road, and on nearby Parliament Street, Mama even added adult family members to "de children God put in me care." She participated in their upkeep and consented to cook meals, which generally meant more chores for me.

Buntin and Wilfred were her nephews, and Mama cooked their dinner for years. Buntin's food was dropped off at his house on Christian Street, and I loved to go there because I would receive some monetary gifts from him. Wilfred picked up his food, but before he even saw his plate or ate his dinner, he would ask, "Dada May, you have any left over?"

She would laugh, appreciating the compliment, and reply, "But you don't even finish eat yet! How you know you need more?"

Job and Linnie were Mama's cousins, perhaps of the same age as Mama. Job was blind, and later, when he lost more independence, Mama cooked his dinners. As a young child, I found pleasure in staring into his eyes when I delivered his food, knowing that he couldn't see me. His eyes were marble grey and moved in quick circles around the sockets.

Linnie, Job's sister, spent most of her time in the mental hospital. Occasionally, when Linnie was doing a little better, Mama sought permission to collect her and moved her into the already cramped house for weeks at a time. As a teenager I wondered why Mama took on a situation like this, but I just could not find a plausible answer. The mind of the young is not as sympathetic or understanding as the mind of the adult. With every visit, Linnie brightened and gained weight under Mama's care. I heard the unusual giggle from Linnie when Mama included her in the house activities and outings, such as washing the clothes, or going to picnics, political meetings, and church services. However, even with all the love and attention from Mama, Linnie would get sick after a while, and Mama had to check her back in the mental home, ready to resume visits the next Sunday.

Having to share some of these responsibilities Mama deliberately took on over the years, I saw that there was nothing easy about raising children. I often wondered why Mama needed to have so many people around her that came with special needs— all ready to extract the endless love she seemed to possess. Now as I think of her life over the years, I ask how much love Mama received in return. Perhaps it did not matter to her anyway; some people are givers.

CHAPTER EIGHT

Mama Is Excited About Education

"...By The Hook Or De Crook..."

EVEN AS I child, I knew that God had blessed me. When I compared my life with that of other children in the neighbourhood, I knew I was blessed to have Mama in my life. Some parents were too busy trying to make ends meet, to waste time on schooling their children. Some children ran around without pants, or in tattered clothes. Some hardly went to school at all, and were very often without books, pencils or other necessities. No doubt the high rate of illiteracy among adults back then was a factor.

But Mama was determined that anyone living under her roof had to attend school, "...by de hook or de crook. Everybody must learn to at least read, write and know how to add and subtract." This was Mama's vow.

There was an appearance of magic in the way Mama managed her affairs, or as the locals would say "turned her hands." Though each of us would have to be deprived in some way for another to benefit, with a child's carefree attitude, I did not wonder too much about the division of resources, nor Mama's ability to provide for my upkeep. Others in the household had similar needs for school supplies, clothes, and other necessities. Nothing was plentiful except sugar cane, mangoes, sweet potatoes and pumpkins in season. As I look back at those times, it was not only about dividing resources: Mama was also consciously living up to the principles she had learned from her own grandmother, Sophie Daniel. Mama had learned about commitment to children, and had learned that education was a necessity.

As a role model, Mama was a good reader and was excellent at arithmetic and penmanship. She and Daddy Edmund were the only two people I can recall ever having a book or newspaper in hand, outside of the neighbours who occasionally read the Bible. I used to sit in her lap as she read the Worker's Voice, the local newspaper, or marveled at how she buried herself in every book I took out of the mobile library or any magazine that strayed into the yard. On Sundays, she devoured the religious pamphlets, and tested how well I had memorized the Golden Text from Sunday school lesson.

"Throw your body in there when you doing something," she encouraged when homework proved difficult. She demonstrated addition and subtraction on any piece of paper, wrote on her leg with a fish bone, or used stones and sticks from the yard as teaching aids for arithmetic problems. For the rudiments of penmanship, her palm engulfed my tiny left hand as she slid my hand into long cursive loops that were typical of her own handwriting—slender and artistic. Most importantly, Mama taught phonetics way before I started formal education.

Mama knew answers to many of the questions in a book entitled The Student's Companion. She recited poems by Alfred Lord Tennyson, Robert Louis Stevenson, and Robert Browning. She was proud of her intelligence, and would tell us stories of the times when she went to school. One day, her teacher Mr. Henry, gave the class a mental arithmetic test. He read a problem, cautioning all of his students to put their pencils down, and then, given an allotted time, students worked the problem mentally, and wrote down the answer. Mama followed the instructions and got all the answers right, only to be admonished by the teacher, because getting all the correct answers made him suspicious. His doubt made Mama angry. "Mr. Henry know I can do me work; it vex me see," she complained.

When I had difficulty in elementary school with long division, our heads merged many times to find the answers. Even though she was exhausted many nights after picking cotton or pounding stones during the off-season of the sugar crop, she found time for us as, one after another, we queued up with our homework. She checked every sum and each word's spelling. She loved mathematical word problems—proportion and simple interest were her specialty.

Mama had a list of goals to accomplish, although none were ever verbalized to us. She employed any means to bring them to fruition.

In a distant corner of the yard, hidden by a border of trees, she raised a perpetual litter of pigs. I hated feeding them, hated the smell of them. Pigs were annoying and filthy. One night, I remember watching the light from the flames of a flambeau, a homemade torch, as it flickered on Mama's face. As an aroma of raw flesh and pig's excreta settled, the mother pig grunted and moaned as Mama's hands moved like a surgeon with an old rag and hot water. A litter of pigs wiggled and squeaked its way into the world. Minutes later, the mother sow settled for the night, with a piglet clinging to each breast for sustenance. Mama's eyes must have danced with the good fortune that these piglets brought: typing classes, confirmation dresses, shoes, and books for all of us.

A pig sold meant extra money for a new pair of church shoes, a harvest hat, or some school clothes. A pig sold meant Mama could throw money towards a hand in the neighbourhood box – a form of community banking. The money collected weekly was given to a single member of the group and was called a "hand." One year, Mama's "hand" financed additional rooms for the house, and paid for textbooks and typing lessons. Shoes and fabric for dresses came out of her bag after shopping trips to St. John's. However, I never felt better about those animals, even though I knew the food on my plate, the new dresses to start school, and the supplies for the rest of my cousins and my brother Eardley, were all a result of their sale.

In 1967, I passed the primary school exam, which ensured my entry to Princess Margaret Secondary School. I assumed Mama didn't want to take the chance that I would be sent home for, God forbid, not having a straw hat or a valise too. I stepped up Gray's Farm Road carrying a small valise stocked with writing books, a ruler, a pen, pencil, eraser and a geometry set. Some of my writing books had come from Mama's older children, now living in the Virgin Islands and America.

Mama beamed like a flashlight on that first morning, fussing over every detail from my socks to my hat. She retied the pink ribbon in my short hair a few times, gave the socks a turn and wished that the sales man at Bata's shoe store had encouraged her to buy a larger size so they would last longer.

Mrs. Mason, Mama's childhood school friend, had made the pink blouse and grey jumper, which was pleated from waist to hemline. I never stopped to wonder how Mama was able to provide all those items from stores around St. John's: the fabric came from Chaia's Store—local Lebanese merchants, elastic and zipper came from Mrs. Wallace's sewing shop, pencils and so on came from Miss Thibou's Bookstore, and shoes came from Bata.

Mama's eyes were glassy with excitement. She fidgeted nervously as if it were her first day at a new school. She twirled me around and for a moment, I saw Mama twirl around too. I did not know then that she was imagining herself going to secondary school. I learned years after that her dream had been to attend the teacher's college. Perhaps that morning she saw some part of herself reflected in me and was proud. Her tireless help and interest with my schoolwork had paid off too.

Everything I ever needed appeared, so I expected the same with this new stage of my life. On the second day, the headmaster, Mr. Basil Peters gave out a booklist. The books totaled $23.06. It sounded exorbitant just for books, but I needed books to learn.

I reasoned out the situation before I got home. Mama had just spent the box money to purchase other items for my schooling, so my uncle, Daddy Edmund, should pay for my books.

Mama was seated at the entrance of the back door shelling peas, a plastic bowl of peas in her lap and a container of shells at her side. The scent of salt beef and chicken for the evening's dinner filled the air.

"Wha! books carn't cost dat much. A way me go get all dat money from?" Daddy Edmund exclaimed when I showed him the list. He had barely finished his question when Mama May spat out a list of commands as if she had rehearsed for this very moment. Lifting her head from the bowl of peas, she focused indignantly on me, though I knew her indignation was not truly about me.

"Chile, go in de bedroom and look under the bed. Behind a white bundle, beside the table, tied up in a red 'kerchief is a $20 US. Change it and buy yuh books." Suddenly, books for secondary school were there, with little effort on my part. The money came from one of her children overseas. Generally such funds were to be reserved for some emergency, such as replacing a neighbour's glass window broken by one of the children, or purchasing a pair of shoes after one of us had unexpectedly mutilated our plastic shit mashers or sandals.

CHAPTER NINE

Mama Shows Forsight

"Learn A Skill. Mek You'self Useful"

MAMA'S PASSION FOR us to be independent adults did not end with formal schooling. She was wise enough to know that not everyone was endowed with equal ability and interest in academics. However, she was sure that with two hands, each of us could learn a skill. With that belief in mind, she was determined that everyone in her household pursue some training for personal development.

Mama believed that every child under her care should be occupied with some worthwhile activity following school hours.

"Every tout, monde, sam, and baggi must do sub'm useful," was her way of communicating this command. "De devil always find work fu idle hands."

Chores like washing dishes, sweeping the yard, and picking up clothes from clotheslines, or filling barrels and sterilized oil drums with water from the public standpipe were standard.

Jerome learned welding, while Elaine and Rhonie were schooled in sewing. Pomroy, Eardley, and Ira studied carpentry, and Fitzroy, Barry and Byron learned woodcraft at a local furniture shop. To keep me from the devil's grasp, Mama unilaterally decided that I should learn to sew.

I wish Mama had checked with me before deciding this, for I saw no residual benefit in going to sewing classes. Carpentry was more beneficial. The boys were bringing home a stool, a bench, or a bookshelf.

I also did not want to sew because I had a hidden inferiority complex about being left handed and knew I could never be successful at sewing for this very reason.

Culturally, left-hand dominance was aggressively discouraged. When babies stretched the left hand (generally referred to as the "wrong" hand) for a piece of food, they were slapped gently but determinedly on the wrist and forced to use the right.

For those of us whose brain resisted the unwiring, we were made to feel handicapped, and branded as "left-handed crabs." There was evidence of my handicap in every move. Each thing I did clearly stated that I was "a born lefty": poor use of a pair of scissors, the inability to draw or cut on a straight line, or catch a ball. As a lefty I was told repeatedly that I lacked dexterity and graceful muscular movements, so I batted right handed in a game of cricket but could not hit a single ball. When I practiced writing with my right hand, I would hear "...crapeau foot ah run dong tung." That is, totally illegible. To further validate the perceived awkwardness of this "unfortunate" appendage, the inventor of the scissor completely ignored us.

"Scissors nah mek for left-hand people," I often heard growing up.

However, lefties were great marksmen in stone fights. We were picked first on a dodge ball team, and declared best artists at exhibition time for our drawings and craft displays.

By the age of twelve, I had had my fill of dresses made by seamstresses over the years: ones made by Mrs. Richards in Greenbay, Mrs. Shannon in Ovals, Miss G in Hatton, and Mrs. Mason in Ottos. Now, I was wearing ready-made dresses, sent by Mama's children who lived abroad. I wondered if Mama knew what it felt like now, to step up Gray's Farm Road on Sundays wearing them. On my way to church, I felt privileged, above my peers who did not wear ready-made dresses, or equal to those who did. These dresses were a symbol of rising status and wealth, and though I knew none of the latter existed for us, these dresses declared to admirers that parcels had been received from someone overseas and that the styles were designed and sewn by persons who were so skillful that they did not have to measure.

At the time, a revolution in clothing was taking place at our house and in Antigua. Ready-made dresses were becoming fashionable, as people migrated and sent clothes back to their families. Both Mama and I were already wearing off-the-rack dresses that were either sent by her children, or given as gifts by her best friend Ms. Lillian, who visited from America. Clothing stores, such as Edris, and Teacher, owned by indigenous Antiguans, were doing brisk business and giving the Syrians, who only sold fabrics, a run for their money. We were all becoming part of the new craze, craving a world outside that of our norm. Everyone wanted to look like the models in the JC Penny and Simplicity catalogues. And though the local seamstresses did their best to copy the styles perfectly, ready-made clothes from Edris and Teacher were feeding our appetites for American wear.

I expected Mama to understand these feelings, for she was part of the changing world too. Kool-Aid, Tang, and Fizzy had replaced fresh lemonade, ginger beer, and sorrel in her household. The barrels of canned goods from overseas were fetched with pride and received the envy of some neighbours. Lawry's and Adobo, powdered seasonings laced with monosodium glutamate, were much more convenient than chopping onions, fresh thyme, and chives. Having to walk to the salt pond near Five Islands Village was a sign of grave poverty. Clearly, Mama's new culinary practices sent a message that she was open to changes and progress. Yet, with sewing, she was locked in a time warp of tape measure, thimble, needle, thread, and Mrs. Mason's old Singer sewing machine.

My apprenticeship in sewing came just at the time of an inevitable rebellion I went through that started in 1967. Many things were happening then. I had recently started secondary school. The pride that came of a walk through the city inflated a child's ego and strengthened the self-assurance and independence Mama had encouraged for years. Yet at twelve, she was still choosing my school shoes, selecting my church hats, and dragging me to every political, trade union, and juvenile Labor Party meeting. As the oldest girl in the house, my responsibilities were many: shopping, cooking on Sundays, and taking food to neighbours. Mama's hair had to be washed, ironed, and combed by me, and I had to dress her for special outings. With the onset of adolescence, I began to wage a war against her continued shadowing, the many household chores, and newly made efforts to turn me into a seamstress.

I couldn't understand Mama's passion for sewing. She was not a seamstress, nor had her daughters become seamstresses. Why waste effort on me? I had seen her put patches on the bottom of the boys' pants, hem dresses, and do needlework on pillowcases for gifts. When Mama May made baby clothes, sewed panties for one of the grandchildren, or put intricate embroidery on pillowcases made from bleaching flour bags, I never heeded her plea to attempt these on my own. I knew a skirt ripped at the waist could be hidden with a few safety pins or made perfectly workable with my crooked stitches. It was not easy to run a needle and thread from left to right with the same dexterity as Mama. All this, coupled with my lame excuse about scissors, and Mama's enthusiasm, made sewing my least favorite past time.

Mrs. Mason, a fine seamstress, was the person elected to instill in me a love of sewing. Mama was excited. Twice a week, I said to Mama, as I bolted through the rusty galvanized gate at the side of the house, "Mama, I'm going to sewing."

She sometimes shouted back, "Chile, take in what Mrs. Mason teaching you. You don't know what privilege you have."

I wasn't learning much. Twice a week, I entered Mrs. Mason's house, said "Good afternoon Mrs. Mason," sometimes played with her daughter, Mercelle, or helped with household chores. Occasionally I ripped seams, basted, or hemmed, but never advanced beyond the basics nor showed any interest in doing so.

I kept my fear of the sewing machine and shame of my left-handedness from Mrs. Mason, but I knew she saw signs of my ineptness. One day, in frustration, I found courage.

"I don't like sewing," I said.

"Child, it's something good to learn," she replied, as she shook loose the threads I had just ripped from a shirt. "You don't like to dress up?"

"Oh yes, Mrs. Mason, but my cousins send ready-made dresses for me from the Virgin Islands," I answered proudly. "I even get clothes from Canada, where Mama has a pen pal."

"You know, child, sometimes you may want to make something so different, that no store in any place has one like it, and then you will feel really special," Mrs. Mason replied. "That is only possible when you can cut and sew for yourself."

But I could not be convinced: the convenience and beauty of ready-made clothing was slowly overtaking the local seamstresses and I thought Mrs. Mason did not know what she was talking about.

One day as I ran a piece of elastic into a seam, she called me into the kitchen. I stood there as she prepared dinner.

"Did you know your Mama and I went to the same school?" she asked.

"Yes, ma'am," I replied. "Mama told me, that's why I am here to learn to sew."

She smiled, "I am sure that's not the only reason she sent you. It's for your own good. I was one of her classmates that stayed in school as long as she did. In those days children left school at an early age to help out at home. But Molly—we called her "Teacher Molly"—when she passed her exams, we all knew she was going to be a teacher."

In her eyes was a sparkle. I could tell they had been good friends back then.

"Mrs. Mason, you are the first person I hear call Mama 'Teacher Molly,'" I said, my eyes wide. I thought of the many times Mama had been able to assist me with homework; she would explain things so logically and clearly. I was able to finally grasp the addition of pounds, shillings and pence when Mama intervened.

"We all used to tell her, 'Molly, you going to be a teacher one day.' She was so bright," Mrs. Mason continued. I sucked in every word. Mama read every library book I brought home, every Nancy Drew,

Hardy Boys, Sunday school tract, and newspaper, but I had never heard anyone talk about Mama's intelligence with such admiration.

"She used to get all her sums right," Mrs. Mason added.

"I know, she knows how to do proportion, simple interest and, can you believe, long division?" The last was another of my mathematical nemeses. Mrs. Mason must have seen the excitement in my eyes—she had captured my total interest.

"Child," Mrs. Mason, who spoke the Queen's English at all times, said. "Most of all, Teacher Molly had the best handwriting among all of us."

Thereafter, I looked forward to the visits in the hopes of learning more about Mama, but still with no interest in learning more about sewing. I spent most of my time helping Mrs. Mason in the kitchen or listening to her talk about her school days and friendship with Mama. Other times we conversed as I did basic sewing tasks, such as ripping seams and pushing elastic through necklines and sleeves. Of course, I was old enough to know that this state of euphoria, this state of deception and lack of progress could not carry on forever. Mama was too astute for the deception to go unnoticed.

One day, Mama received a parcel from her pen pal in Canada. Mrs. Wagner was a white woman who had advertised her desire for a pen pal in a local newspaper in Antigua. It was a popular custom in those days for people to write to each other sharing customs and culture. Mama had insisted that I have a pen pal, too, and so for years I wrote to a girl from America named Cathy Boule. Mrs. Wagner was kind, occasionally sending money for Mama's birthday and Christmas. Sometimes the clothes sent were too heavy for Antigua's climate but Mama always showed gratitude. "It's the thought that counts," she'd say, "Ah didn't give her anything to put up."

Mama instructed me to try on one of the dresses she had just received. It was the correct size but needed a few inches shaved from the hem. "Chile if you cut a piece from the hem that should be good for church on Sunday." Now, all this time, I had not touched a scissors at Mrs. Mason's. Faced with the challenge of cutting a straight line across a dress sent from Canada, I realized I needed to extricate myself from this predicament.

I looked in Mama's eyes with all the sincerity I could muster and said, "Mama, you know scissors not made for left-handed people."

"Chile, so you didn't learn to use the scissors all this time. What you learning all this time?" Mama demanded.

I couldn't answer. Mama insisted that I cut and hem the dress, and however it turned out, I would have to wear it. Appalled by the crooked strip that I eventually chopped off, and the large stitches—"even a blind man can see"—Mama soon called a halt to my sewing trade.

As I shamefully walked to church that Sunday, Mama must have finally concluded that I lacked the interest to learn how to sew and that my left hand was never going to cut a straight piece of cloth. In time, she would refine my ability to at least hem pants, dresses, and darn—a set of skills she termed "...enough sewing to save yuh life."

Later, I learned that she, too, was sent to learn to sew by her Grandmother Sophie. Unlike me, Mama had the interest, loved sewing, and wanted to make clothes for friends. However, the seamstress who felt threatened by Mama's eagerness and quickness never cut a pattern in her presence. Though Mama did not use the sewing machine, she still taught me the little she knew and, like any good parent, simply wanted me to accomplish more than she had. If only I could have fulfilled this dream of hers. This is one of my regrets later in life and remains so up to this day. With a talent for drawing and an interest in design, I have often wished I could sew. But I could not see it then. I was too young to understand parental foresight. Left-handedness, poor hand-eye coordination, and the one-sided design of scissors were obstacles that could be overcome for future benefits.

One of the sayings in Antigua is that "Crapeau no walk and dem pickney jump." Mama had stepped over obstacles racing through life, functioning not only on instinct, but also on tradition.

Part of her intuition came from the journey of her grandmother Sophie, and other people's journeys before that. Back then, most girls learned to sew, and this had been so for generations. I was ignorant to the history of Mama's stamina and perseverance, and could not understand that her journey now included me, and that every parenting triumph was, in her eyes, a seed planted that would someday bear fruit.

May Ambrose (*Photo 1983*)

Sitting: Mama May's mother, Frances Grant (Pepsi) surrounded by grandchildren (Sam Mike's daughters) (L-R) Janice, Debbie, Sharon and baby Junie. (*Photo 1965.*)

Joseph Ambrose, (Grandpa): Mama's father (*Photo 1970*)

Mama May's sister, Ruth Allen with granddaughter
Francine Lloyd. (*Photo 1969*).

Mama & Her Children: Rear (L-R): Ira Tittle, Rhonie Edwards, Eardley Tittle, Elaine Tittle, Jerome Tittle, Fitzroy Tittle **(Standing in back of Mama May)**, the author Monica Tittle (8 years old) **Front (L-R)**: Rhonda James(Mama's great niece), Barrymore (Barry) Tittle, Mama May Ambrose, Mama's grandsons Anderson Nesbitt (Baby Andy) and Dave Smith. *(Photo 1964)*

Edmund Tittle (Daddy Edmund) (*Photo 1988*)

St. John's Anglican Cathedral.
Photo courtesy Adelaja Olatunji

Samuel Mike (Mama May's younger brother) with his
great-nephew Michael Perry in Canada
(Photo dated 2008)

Family Photo of Byron & Carolyn Tittle's wedding, Bronx, New York. Mama May is sitting next to the bride playing her usual role as nurturer with 2 children in her arms. On Mama's left is her lifelong companion, Jacob Tittle (Daddy Edmund). (*June 23, 1990*).

Monica Matthew with Mama May. *Summer 1999*

May Ambrose 2001

Cassada Gardens #2
St John's
Antigua. 24. 1. 2000

Hello Monica,

Greeting in Jesus precious name, I am just writing you these few lines, to tell you, I received the things from Hunston, and was glad to do so I thank you very much for the interest you have taken in me, I wish you all the best for the future kiss your Grandson for me and tell the two children hello, how is Gloria tell her plenty howdy for me, and hope she is feeling much better.

Dudley brought a nice cake for my birthday I enjoyed it very much, Please excuse my writing you know, I am not young as before Say hello to Gloria daughter for me, although I do not know her.

I am
as always, Mama

At the time Mama penned this letter on January 24, 2000,
she was 80 years old.

CHAPTER TEN

Apathy

"Blood Thicker Than Water"

ANY PARENTS IN Gray's Farm yearned for their children to escape the labels attached to their locality as lacking in industry, poor, and unintelligent.

In reality, most of the residents, just like Mama, worked daily, set high standards, and educated their children. Gray's Farm, now called Gray's Green Community, has produced teachers, doctors, lawyers, artists, mechanics, writers, calypsonians, musicians, and, as of 2004, Antigua's third Prime Minister. The community has a legacy of pride and perseverance in the face of adversity. It has the longest running sport's club—The Empire Football Club—and has made the biggest contributions to the development of cricket and football in Antigua over the years. It is the most politically astute of all the constituencies on the island, voting representatives out of office for inefficiency regardless of political party affiliation.

Mama was always trying ways to make life a little better for us. She was a member of The Anglican Church Society (the major benefit was a waiver of the burial fee). We attended church and Sunday School most Sundays. Mama was actively involved in political, trade union, and singing groups. Girl Guides and Girl Scouts were added prestige.

As a Girl Guide, my many efforts to gain badges were not successful. With my left-handedness, the task of making knots and other skills proved daunting. Nevertheless, I visited the tallest point in Antigua, Boggy Peak. We hiked in the woods, learned survival skills, such as how to light a fire with only one match, and learned how to apply first aid to treat sprains and broken limbs. My proudest moment was wearing the well-starched and ironed Guide uniform in a parade to greet Queen Elizabeth II's during her visit to Antigua in 1966 during our Statehood celebration. Marching like young military women raised our self-esteem. That uniform represented status and discipline. Mama knew that activities of this nature would benefit any young girl. I was finally becoming aware of the intense love that was nourished daily by Mama's continued commitment to me. But, I had yet to understand how love, though acknowledged, could be simultaneously ignored.

Typing was a privilege, and a sacrifice. To send a child to typing lessons in those days meant economic sacrifice. It required resourcefulness. For both parent and child, the pride and potential benefits of learning to type eclipsed the extra monetary efforts required. So, I was sent to Miss Simon's Typing School at the bottom of Gray's Farm Road. I stepped down Gray's Farm Road proudly with a large typing manual. I passed my old elementary school and continued to Miss Simon's house, a stone's throw away. In my young mind, I was the envy of the other girls whose parents were not as ambitious as Mama May.

Still, it was a struggle, and ironically, it was my right hand that posed the difficulty. As a strong left-hander, it was an arduous task to break in my right fingers to equal usage, and my hand-eye coordination was not instinctive. To develop the discipline, I practiced "asdf" and ";lkj" hundreds of times, and filled pages with this odd combination of letters. Miss Simon insisted all eyes be kept on the typing tablet, not on the keys, but I was convinced that, because of the way my brain was wired, this was the most difficult thing to do. In time, I developed speed and accuracy. With Mama's encouragement and persistence, I persevered. She was making the monetary sacrifice already, perhaps by denying herself a new dress, or dipping into the rainy day monies sent by my overseas relatives.

At the time I did not consider the fact that I was the only one of the children who was sent to typing lessons.

Typing was a success, even though I lacked the skill to compete with the enthusiasts who typed above 65-80 words per minute. I mastered 45 words with few mistakes to pass my first London Institute of Typing exam. Since then, those lessons have proved invaluable. I have blessed Mama's insightfulness time and time again, particularly when I attended The Antigua Teachers' Training College, and later New York City Technical College. I was quite proud to be able to submit typed reports.

Whenever I reflect on my days of going to typing lessons, one of my wars with Daddy Edmund comes to mind. In fact, it was a war with Mama, too.

Daddy Edmund hid behind a veneer of sternness, but that was also his way of protecting us. My pleasant memories with him go back to an early time: I was five years old and riding with him on a donkey through the capital city of St. John's, to the child nursery on Dickenson Bay Street. We stopped at the market a few times to drink coconut water or to suck on oranges, and people would admire the man with the child in his arm seated on a donkey. He rode sidesaddle with one of his arms wrapped around my little body, while the other held the bit extending from the donkey's mouth. My cousins and I knew he loved us, even though men generally assumed a role that was intimidating, aloof, and unemotional. We felt privileged that he was a part of our lives, for having a man's presence around was certainly not the norm in many homes in Gray's Farm.

Growing up, Grandpa and Daddy Edmund attached labels to us based on our flaws. Fitzroy was "own-way," which meant he was always out of the yard without permission, hanging around with friends at the beach or at the football grounds. Barry, the surviving twin, was big bellied, had too many friends and was easily influenced, which meant that he was "dung gut" and "own-way," too. I was "brazen and stubborn." I doubted the accuracy of such an unfair description, for the same was said about most young people then, but the phrase was thrown at me so frequently that it actually started to feel good to be brazen and stubborn. I used to stare down Daddy Edmund deliberately, convinced that that was the way to communicate. Look a person in the eye when you speak I had heard. Not so with Daddy Edmund. Looking him in the eye was interpreted as rude and insolent. To me, it was intense listening! It was repeatedly said, "Children should be seen and not heard." Not with me—I deserved the right to be heard even when the conflict involved Daddy.

We all knew his wrath, and believed that he was trained to war against children. His motto was "be prepared to give a whipping." That was why, when it came to matters with my uncle, Mama had two warnings for me: "pick your wars carefully," and "blood thicker than water."

One morning, after I had dressed for typing, Daddy Edmund decided that I was not to wear the new pair of yellow patent leather sandals I had selected, the ones that had recently arrived in a parcel from St. Thomas. Those sandals were the latest fashion and, that Saturday morning, I was determined to wear them to my typing lesson. At thirteen, it seemed that attending secondary school certainly came with some degree of maturity. I felt I had earned the privilege of selecting my own clothes, without consultation. However, wearing church shoes to any place besides church was equal to breaking one of the Ten Commandments: church things were for church. There were church hats, church clothes, church bags; the list goes on and on, but these shoes were not church shoes. Therefore, Daddy Edmund had no conceivable reason to object, and I wanted to feel the gratification of wearing my new sandals that morning, not another day.

I left the house with the sandals tucked under my dress. Seconds after clearing the gate, I removed the pair of old tennis shoes I was wearing and tucked them under a large stone pillar on the side of Grandpa's house. Soon after, I stepped down Gray's Farm Road like Mama on Easter Sunday, my yellow sandals dazzling in the morning sun.

Upon my return, I saw Daddy Edmund waiting in the center of the yard, the pair of old tennis shoes in one hand and a curled up piece of old leather belt in the other. Instinctively, I prepared for battle and looked around for an ally. Mama was a few feet away, sitting over a bath pan of clothes and sporting her usual pout. I knew she had always drawn a line on matters that involved my uncle and me in the past, but I never lost hope that she would be brave enough to defend me one day. It was at such times, though, that she disavowed her right as my adopted mother to protect me. At such times, she would say, "blood thicker than water, ah not stepping in." She would remind Daddy Edmund, though, that I was his niece, his "dead brother chile." Though I knew these were her pleas for mercy, I felt disdain and contempt at those words – equal to the contempt I felt for my uncle. These were the times I recalled that she was not my biological mother and all that we had worked on over time became diminished in the face of the simple fact that he was blood, and she was not.

Whenever I was disciplined or teased, I had the exclusive right to my dead parents. It drove me to draw power from these two dead people who had left this world by the time I was four years old. I claimed a disadvantaged position on that ground—there ought to be some benefit, after all, to the constant reminders of their status over the years. Mama's apathy left me with no other choice. I was now alone in this world, so I collected courage, silently swearing to a dead mother and father that Daddy Edmund was not going to make me cry this time.

There was the familiar glare in his eyes whenever one of us got a beating.

"Why you disobey me and wear de new shoes?"

He and I both knew that no answer would be satisfactory enough to prompt him to put away the leather belt, dim the heat in his eyes, and sit on a chair under a tree to admire the sunshine. Nothing could slake his need for a beating but giving a beating.

I stared back at him, feeling no desire to give an answer. I was filled with anger over the fact that simply wearing a pair of sandals, my own sandals, had brought on this battle. I stood defiantly, like David ready for Goliath. Mama jabbed at the clothes, head still bowed, looking Lilliputian behind the tub. Daddy Edmund pounced like a raging bull, locking one half of my body between his side and a hairy arm.

"You too stubborn and brazen," he raged, the familiar label bouncing off my ears. "You listen to nobody. Dis will teach you a lesson."

I could see Mama's face now, slightly raised, but still passive. It was as if her body had been glued to the bench. I read the words in her eyes, "blood thicker than water." I glared at her. Where are you now when I need you, Mama? Defend me against this man! This was not a war I picked — I only wore a pair of shoes. My mind was racing with thoughts. You have often defended me from the occasional sibling fights, quickly warned a neighbour's child not to interfere with me, but Daddy Edmund has all the freedom. The sadness in your eyes is not sufficient — come to my rescue! Nothing! Mama sat there, indifferent, apathetic to my plight, disengaged from my war.

I did not make a sound. Channeling all my resentment, I distanced myself from the pain of the belt across my back, biting hard into my lips at every blow that landed there. My uncle did not deserve my tears. I felt redeemed by the frustration on his face. He huffed and puffed from the struggle and I hissed involuntarily, my chest lifting in time with the slight tremors of my lower jaw. I projected the hurt and anger onto Mama when I looked at her, paralyzed, all in the name of blood.

"Edmund, mind de girl eye, remember she yuh dead brother chile," she uttered. And my blood curled. I yearned for her to defend me more aggressively, not from a distance.

When he released me, I staggered backwards, yet there was still enough defiance left in me to give a retort.

"You had no right to hit me, I wear what was mine!" I cried. "You beat me because I have no mother and father."

Mama May raised her head higher, perhaps shocked that I had the gumption to give "back talk," and perhaps shocked too, by my denial of her status as my mother.

I would later learn that Mama had good reason to keep her distance and that her warning to pick my wars carefully was a lesson she had learned on her own. When her daughter, Elaine, was a teenager, Mama warned Elaine not to wear her church shoes to school. When she told Daddy Edmund about Elaine's disobedience, Mama's intention was simply for him to give a warning. Elaine knew the rules. Church shoes for church and school shoes for school.

Daddy Edmund held on to Elaine, "beating her as if she killed somebody," were Mama's exact words. How could Mama forget how much his hands itched for our backsides? He took turns with us as if we were his personal muscle toner. Daddy Edmund was from a different school of corporal punishment, a place where he was convinced that such actions would make us more obedient. Some parents believed love existed in that place and expected an outpour from a child after a beating. Daddy Edmund continued to thrash Elaine, so Mama interjected.

"Edmund, dat's enough man, she didn't kill anybody!"

But he could not snap out of his abusive stupor, and consequently, Mama, yielding to a mother's instinct to protect and save, grabbed the nearest piece of wood and struck him on the shoulder. As if in slow motion, he released Elaine, and picked up a plank. His hand and plank came up and down on Mama's head. Consciousness left her body, before her weight hit the ground.

This story, told to me many years after my own fateful beating, brought a reemergence of sadness and anger to both of us.

"I didn't know he was going to beat her," she said.

For all the years growing up with Mama, this was the first time I learned that Daddy Edmund had physically abused her. The term "physical abuse" sounded harsh, so I struggled to find another dressing to cover this old sore that plagued women in Gray's Farm for years. How society had programmed us, I thought, from the law to the church to the medical sector. Women learned to function with such secrets and many remained hidden but not forgotten. And Mama was one of these women.

That was the reason she refused marriage all those years.

I felt guilty for reminding her about her silence during my wars with Daddy Edmund. How could I now ask her to explain why at certain times she would remind me "blood thicker than water"? I could not let her know that her axiom diminished our relationship. "Water" in our vernacular sometimes symbolized something of little value: "watery soup" was not tasty, had no substance; "throw water on that" spoke of denying the existence of something. I wanted to be "blood" in relation to Mama at all times, for that was where security existed, that was where love lived. How could I tell her at that time that I felt abandoned?

I was able, however, to understand as an adult, given the added information she provided, and I surmised that Mama picked the wars she could win.

CHAPTER ELEVEN

The Precious Lesson Of Trust

"I Trust You To Do The Right Thing"

NEVER UNDERSTOOD and never asked why Daddy Edmund, who was such a major part of our lives, lived next door in a small house by himself. It seemed a strange arrangement, but he was near enough to cross Grandpa's yard to discipline and enforce the rules Mama relegated to him.

Daddy Edmund's presence ensured extra food, money, and during crop seasons, there were ground provisions such as sugar cane, sweet potatoes, white yams, pumpkins, squashes, cassava, and always the aroma of mangoes ripening in a corner. However, Daddy Edmund whipped us for any and every reason: whenever we failed to fetch water from the standpipe, if we pouted, or gave 'back talk, if we forgot to sweep the yard, if we failed to say good morning, if we forgot to say good afternoon, and if we stood too close to him when someone was getting a whipping. What I feared the most, though, was the way he doused us with medicinal concoctions approved by Mama: Sulfur Bitters, Senna, Scott's emulsion, worm syrup, castor oil, Epsom salts, and cod liver oil.

He was not tall by any means, but on Saturday mornings, he lengthened in the center of the yard, a head, on a neck, in awe of itself, and a handsome but cadaverous face with jaws sunken into the hollows carved by missing teeth.

Mama would pass him the wide-mouthed bottle of cod liver oil.

"Hey, come!" he would say. My stomach coiled and his handsomeness disappeared as he perched on an old piece of tree trunk.

In seconds, my tiny body writhed in his arms, as he held my nose shut. I was determined not to swallow; he vowed to force the foul cod liver oil over my teeth, inside my jaws, tongue, lips, and down my throat.

"Swallow Monica, and get it over with," Mama would urge from behind him.

Of course, Daddy Edmund succeeded every time, sometimes administering another dose after I had spat the mixture all over my nightgown. I had no choice but to swallow it eventually. It moved slowly, moving from my lips and teeth, to the inside of my jaws, then sliding away from my tongue, crawling sluggishly to my throat, slithering down the esophagus, and then sat in my stomach, only to resurface with every belch.

"Why do I have to drink this fishy stuff?" I asked Mama one day.

"It's good for your skin and eyes."

"But I still get rashes, and you still wear glasses. Did you drink cod liver oil when you were little?" I asked.

"Chile, you ask a lot of question nuh? You still have sores because your blood too sweet—you eat too much candy— and I wear glasses because I'm getting older; it has nothing to with cod liver oil."

She paused for a while to tie her head with a colourful head cloth and assess what she had said, then added, "As far as I can remember, all children get cod liver oil in Antigua; it's a custom."

"So this oil, this is just habit? Didn't you tell me not to follow things other people do, Mama?"

She smiled, "Chile, they send you fu me." That expression meant I had asked too many questions. "You testing me patience," she continued. "Ask your uncle."

But I ventured, "I can't wait to stop taking it."

She chuckled, but on my face was a serious protestation. "Mama, it makes me want to vomit. The taste never leaves my mouth!"

"It not so bad you know, chile. Next time I give you a piece of orange or lime but you can't let your uncle see. You know how he say I spoil you."

I think she was relieved to have him perform the unpleasant aspects of parenting.

Daddy Edmund also mistrusted all young people. When these conflicts arose, and I complained to Mama, she would say, "…see, I trust you to do the right thing."

Unlike Mama, Daddy Edmund trusted no young girl once she reached teenage years. I never understood this sudden switch, for he and I trusted each other when I was younger. I washed, dyed his hair black and twisted little braids in it for fun.

Parents felt that children needed an extra scrubbing from time to time, so a bath from parents was customary across Antigua. When it was my turn, I would have water warming in the sun and Daddy Edmund would scrub all over my body, except for my private areas.

After he was satisfied that rolls of dirt had been removed from my neck, back of my hands and legs, he declared, "Go wash the rest you'self," leaving me to finish as he walked back to his house. I felt clean, safe, and cared for. By the time I reached the age of ten, he no longer felt the need to give a "scrubbing." He now trusted that I could care for myself.

My conflicts with Daddy Edmund started a few years later. Everything about the 70's scared the hell out of my uncle: the hipster and bell-bottom pants, the popcorn-like fabric that hugged the curves of my adolescent body, and my male school friends like Everton, Jesse and Fitzroy. These boys came to the yard for me to braid their hair for a big fluffy afro. I sported an afro too. Calypso songs sung by Lord Short Shirt were social commentaries that addressed the wrongs of the political party that Daddy Edmund and Mama supported. Such songs, and the term "Black Power," could not be spoken in Daddy's presence.

I appeared regularly on a youth radio show called Youth Power, along with friends such as the late C Jacks, Pat Meade, Gene Nanton, Harold Lovell, Andy Omarde, and Glen Richards. We talked about important issues, such as apartheid in South Africa, and the role women were playing in the struggle. I was learning cultural dance steps with Zucan, and Hugh on drums, performing in drama groups with Chaku, and singing on Christmas choirs with Luther and Rosie.

Sightings of me with boys, further fed Daddy Edmund's distrust. He fought my hormonal turmoil, independence of spirit and rebellion to his authority with whippings, which were sure to follow late returns after hanging out with my friends, Helen Mae and Rhonie, and after cultural meetings.

I sensed that adolescence created fear in my uncle, because he had less control. That was when the conflicts began with his daughter Elaine. A decade earlier, Elaine suffered her periods of beatings about boyfriends, and the styles of her clothing. Now, with my adolescence, I automatically became the new tour of duty.

Very often, Daddy Edmund objected to Mama's liberal parenting and overruled a decision she made. For instance, after planning for a school picnic all week, one for which I had gotten permission, Daddy would suddenly declare the day of the picnic that I was not to go. I argued and cried, unable to understand his change of mind, and wished that Mama was bold enough to plead my cause.

Love was what I felt from Mama. Love in those days was never abundant, so the only love I felt could not be gambled with and I was learning not to take it for granted. By the time I was about fourteen years old, I knew how love felt, what it was and how to react to it. Love shielded me from the wrath of a sibling. Love provided the most beautiful dress for confirmation in the Anglican Church. Love bought that special outfit to wear to a school fete, so I could feel as privileged as all my friends. Love made sure that vacations from school were spent in other environments such as the countryside with Grandmother Annie, or with Sister Yvonne in St. Phillips and St. Croix, and later in St. Thomas with Rhonie and Elaine. Love found the money so that I could be registered for my General Certificate Exams to end high school. When I wanted to return to do A Levels Exams, love said I should do so, while Daddy Edmund declared that I should find work to do.

Mama was always ready to defend me against a harsh word from a cousin, or a neighbour who had interpreted my adolescent attitude as "ungrateful to May, you go bite off she ear." There was this strong sense of self that Mama's actions fed in me. Knowing that I was precious in her sight was good medicine for my self-esteem. It helped to build self-confidence and that feeling often kept me in line. Most important was the trust that developed between Mama and me. Trust was the vehicle by which she transmitted her moral values and by doing so it became my guiding light against peer pressure during adolescence.

Somewhere in time, it had become Mama's belief that I would not ever steal or lie to her. It was knowledge of that belief that prevented me from disappointing her. Very often money disappeared from under a pillow, a mattress, or box where she had hidden it away, and Mama questioned everyone in the house but never asked if I had taken it. Consequently, I never did, for I knew that I could not look her in the face and deny I had done it.

Mama never discussed sex with me. I hardly think any parent did at that time. At some point, I was made aware that my body was sacred and was solely my responsibility. Once this had been established, it was left up to me to show that I understood the implications. This trust was reinforced by the way she allowed me the freedom to participate in extracurricular activities. On the other hand, some parents kept their girls under constant watch, not allowing them to participate in cultural activities, yet were dumbfounded when sightings of them with boys came to light or when there was an occasional pregnancy.

When I was sixteen years old, I was tempted to become sexually active. It was an image of Mama's face that extinguished the fire raging in me. I told the boy after a few kisses that I could not go through with it.

"Why, I won't let anyone know," he tried to assure me.

I turned to him and replied emphatically, "Mama will know!"

That thought was my inherent belief, as silly as it sounded. Mama possessed no psychic powers to read my mind, but the guilt and disappointment from deception would have been evident.

CHAPTER TWELVE

Mama And Her Work

"Nobody go hungry on my watch."

M AMA MAY'S WORK at the Antigua Sugar Factory spanned forty years. During that time, children were born, the house was extended to three bedrooms, grown children immigrated to the United States and to the Virgin Islands, and grandchildren arrived for care and love.

From 1935 to 1970, Mama performed a wide range of jobs within the industry, everything from pounding stones for road construction, to picking up loose sugar cane that had fallen from the train trolleys. She also served as a line cook when the harvested sugar cane was loaded onto trolleys.

Line cooks were hired to prepare the workmen's meals. Mama stood on the side of the road or just off the path of the train tracks—locally called "loco lines"—and stooped over twenty pots on a makeshift stove, which was just two long pieces of iron poles with wood from nearby trees cut for fire.

Each day the men brought in the raw ingredients according to what they desired to eat. There was no set menu to reduce the variety of dishes that could be requested. On any day, the list could stretch from rice with peas, plain rice, seasoned rice, sugar fungee or fungee without sugar, or fungee with okras, soup with pigtail, soup with salted beef or chicken. The possibilities went on and on. Individual pots were the order of the day, and over the years Mama had to perfect her skill at combining similar requests in order to reduce the toil, frequently slipping out an unwanted ingredient here and there before presenting it to the workman. She laughed one day when I asked her about these shortcuts and would not reveal her trade secrets.

"Is like dey want to turn me crazy over de different pots," she complained. Yet, amidst the laboring, and eyes red from the smoke of green wood, she found time to teach lessons and to laugh. Food and humour came home with her daily. The food safe, a cabinet made of fine meshed wire and pine wood, contained the week's groceries and any extra flour, sugar, and cornmeal Mama had "cut and contrived" from the workmen.

She had learned how to make good of any situation from her Grandie Sophie, and to justify her actions, she explained, "If three men bring half pound a cornmeal each, how three men can eat pound and half cornmeal of fungee, you know how cornmeal swell?" These extras served us as well as the neighbours, with whom Mama shared the ingredients.

Outside of the gastronomical benefits, Mama's job provided stories that brought levity to the household and to neighbours on hot, dark evenings. Her stories could turn a dismal moment into a roar of laughter. Her voice permeated the night's air, as the women visited our yard with great expectations. Some sat in a circle on plastic buckets, others on the large flat stone in the front of the house, as Mama told stories about her work.

Mama's performance usually started when someone requested a story about the workmen. They had heard the stories many times before.

"Eh Miss May, wha the cheapskate Mr. Phillip say when he bring he lunch again?" Over and over again I heard the story of Mr. Phillip, and every time I looked forward to the new twists and turns Mama would inject in the stories to keep the audience entertained.

"Miss May, I want all me food that ah bring in,' " Mama would say mockingly. The memory lit up Mama's face, while the women lapped their wide skirts between huge legs trying to gain their composure. Mr. Phillip knew that she stretched some men's food to give a meal to others, those of whom did not have lunch.

"Some of de men had plenty mouths to feed; deh hand to mouth and scarcely that." This was her usual saying when someone was struggling to meet family obligations. "You know, nobody go hungry on my watch. Not when me over that huge fire all morning," she declared to the cooing women.

"Ah know you can stretch a few barley loaves Miss May," Miss Chrissie declared, referencing a biblical parable.

"Every mouth shall be fed," someone shouted in a church-like refrain.

"What is a little food?" Mama replied chuupsing—sucking her teeth—with a pout. Her belly shook as she continued the story of Mr. Phillip, making it more dramatic as the women laughed.

Mama related that during lunchtime at the factory, when the men had halted about noon from unpacking cane, they washed up and approached the "kitchen" area.

On this day, Mr. Phillip's meal was salt fish, white dumplings, and spinach. Earlier, when Mama had received his bag of raw ingredients, the contents appeared strange. The foreman was in earshot and had heard Mr. Phillip's request.

"Miss May, ah want all me food that ah bring in," Mama said as she imitated Mr. Phillip. Mama wasn't pleased with what he said, but it was reasonable.

"He want all of whatever he wife pack for him, so I say to meself, finally, ah go give him whatever his wife packed today."

Mr. Phillip came forward after some of the men had collected their lunch. Mama handed him the lunch in a huge enamel pie dish and smiled inwardly. He looked at his food in shock.

"De salt fish was still tie up with the burlap string, like a Christmas present," Mama roared. She had prepped it with onion, tomato paste, and oil, the way Antiguans make it, except that nobody cooks salted dried fish tied up.

At this point the women were lost in a roar of exaggerated coos and Antiguan belly-jerk laughter. Children who could not join in adult conversation, turned sideways and laughed. As the women folded the wide skirts between their legs, Mama recalled the foreman's reaction to Mr. Phillip's complaint.

"I hear you say you want all you food, ah the best way to sure that you get all. Loose de string, man." The women were now off the large stone, buckets, and pails, their bare feet stomping the ground and bodies moving as if in a choreographed fashion.

On a different evening the story was about another of Mama's patrons— "greedy and meaneastic" Mr. Ford, as Mama often called him.

"Ah never see a man that know how much he cornmeal or rice should swell to," she said to the women. He challenged her often saying that she had pinched his ingredients.

"Miss May, half pound cornmeal give a bigger ball ah fungee man," or another time he would say, "...you mean to say de rice couldn't full up de dish?" He lost the argument every time, so he decided to change his strategy.

"Miss May, leave me food in de pot," he began requesting, but Mama would forget and have it all well presented in his light blue flowered enamel bowl, which was said to be as large as a donkey trough.

Mama joked, "Ah never see somebody eat out a bigger dish."

Mr. Ford was relentless. "Miss May, ah say leave me food in the pot."

One day he finally got his pot packed to the rim with seasoned rice. Mama watched the sweat trail down the sides of his face as he ate nearly a pound of rice. She thought "Mmm, mmm, what a greedy man."

The next day, seated on the ground under a mango tree, he consumed a five-pound Glow Spread saucepan of soup made with ground provisions and dumplings, which were called droppers. He belched loudly. Finally, Mama decided to teach Mr. Ford a lesson. The next day, his lunch was fungee and fish, the perfect dish for Mama's plan.

Mama later explained to the foreman."He say leave his food in de pot every day. You don't have to tell me to do nothing over and over for toooo long," she said, smiling.

It wasn't a good idea to leave fungee to sit in a pot. Mama compounded matters by deliberately cooking the cornmeal and water mixture about two hours before lunch. The women sat around her, swept in by Mama's craftiness and drowning in tears brought on by laughter.

"Cousin Miss May, no kill me t'day," Miss Chrissie screamed between laughter.

Mama joked, "Look, by lunch time, me dear, the fungee had on a jacket and tie," meaning that the starchy Antiguan dish had thickened and formed a hard surface. It clung to the side of the pot, cold, unpalatable, and unattractive.

"Miss May, you ah one proper han'," someone declared.

"Oh God Miss May," Mr. Ford said to Mama, "you could ah roll the fungee man!"

Mama quickly and sarcastically replied, "No, ah want to make you see you get all you fungee, man."

The women continued their laughter way into the pitch dark night.

By the time I accompanied Mama to work one day, at the age of eleven, I was armed with abundant descriptions about the men in the work gang. I walked beside her on Bendals Road, privileged to be in her company. I had reveled in the excitement earlier that morning: the dress laid out the night before, white Bata tennis shoes, and a hat for the midday sun. We had hurried up Gray's Farm Road when it was still dark, the morning dew tasting clean and fresh when we boarded a bus at the West Bus Station.

Later, at the sugar cane depot, the trail tracks meandered, and cars stood ready to be packed with heaps of cane delivered by tractors or donkeys from the surrounding fields. The dust from the stone crushing at the Bendals Quarry fogged the valley in the distance. The work gang was located there for the next few weeks. After this time they would move on again to another location and Mama would go too, "stove and all."

I watched in awe as Mama prepared meals for nearly twenty-five men, while bent over a fireside. I counted about eighteen saucepans. At noon, the men piled around to collect their food and sat under nearby trees. They all appeared contented.

Mr. Phillip was still a patron, though having learned his lesson, not to tie his food again. Mr. Ford, however, had remained angry with Mama, and requested a transfer to another work gang to be with another cook.

Looking back, I realize that this invitation to work with Mama was more than just a day off from school, or an opportunity to receive monetary gifts of twenty-five or fifty cents pieces from the workmen. It was a chance for me to see Mama's independence, intelligence, pride in her work, and kindness. As she labored over the fire, thick lines of smoke wafting in all directions, I knew this was her way of teaching by doing, as she had experienced in the past with her own grandmother.

For years, I continued to help her unpack bags and consolidate ingredients. I felt no sense of guilt, for Mama never showed any either. What she took from the men was never for selfish reasons. It was not only for family. She shared some of it with the neighbours and with those persons whom she often said, "might drop by." And they did drop by and were fed. But due to her philanthropic nature, Mama also made sure that meals were delivered to those who could not drop by themselves.

CHAPTER THIRTEEN

Mama Cares For Others

"Someone Might Drop By..."

"WHY YOU HAVE to leave food in the pot Mama?" I asked one day.

"Someone might drop by chile," was always the reply.

Lord knows there were times of insufficiency. I would look at the small ration of fish on my plate and noticed that Daddy's fish swam in sauce in a separate bowl. One day I was so dissatisfied with my piece of chicken that I informed Mama that in my nutrition class at Princess Margaret School, Mrs. Hurst had said children needed more protein than grown adults.

"So, what that mean?" she asked.

"Children should get a larger piece of meat than adults because they're still growing and need protein for growth and repair of tissues." It was memorized straight from my notes. Once Mama realized that protein meant "meat kind," there was a short pause as she mentally weighed the size of fish, meat, or chicken on a child's plate against that on the adult's plate.

Finally, she responded, "Oh yeah? You tell Mrs. Hurst, dat me May say, when she bring home de 'meat kind' in this house, you will get a bigger piece."

We both laughed together at her witty response. But there was never much laughter when it was my favorite meal. At those times, that "someone who might drop by" was not a welcome guest. Once Mama thought you had your fair share she would give a verbal scolding saying, "be satisfied with what you get; be contented."

Where food was concerned, Mama was not like some of the neighbours. Very often a playmate lingered until dinnertime just to share a meal, or a neighbour engaged in conversation on local politics, would stay longer than necessary, knowing a little food would be available at the end of the visit. When I would visit my friends' homes, their mothers would call them in for dinner, but let me know it was time to go home.

"Chile, go to Miss May, she must be wondering 'bout you."

I do not think they were necessarily being mean. Some just did not have enough to share, while others were intimidated by Mama's reputation as a good cook and did not want to expose themselves as otherwise. Occasionally, I was happy for such a command because it saved me from eating in some homes. Everybody knew whose mother cooked rice with "water running one way," or whose fungee had "friends" (referring to lumps of uncooked cornmeal), or whose fungee "ate short" (which meant it was undercooked). Even in those challenging times, there were still standards.

Those of Mama's friends who could not drop by were still fed. Much to my chagrin, the responsibility to deliver food to them fell into my lap. While my friends played ring games, marbles, dollhouse, or hopscotch on sunny afternoons until dinnertime, I brought food to a slew of people. The jeers were piercing whenever I passed with a food carrier containing someone's dinner or a pail to collect scraps of food for the pigs.

Added to this, I was beginning to feel the urge to rebel against Mama's constant presence in my life. Children assume they can swim without fins and fly without wings. I was under Mama's watch most of the time: after youth meetings she'd be there to collect me, and at adult meetings, I was there with her. The undemocratic way in which she had chosen sewing for my developmental skill, knowing I was left-handed, continued to be a thorn in my side. The free reign that my cousin Fitzroy enjoyed, because he was a boy, caused me to detest my regular food delivery trek up Greenbay Hill to Mama's friend, Mr. Foster. His wife, Ms. Lillian, was Mama's best friend, and she had migrated to America.

There were other reasons to hate the trip. For a girl, Gray's Farm and its environs were not the safest places to walk around. I had to carefully avoid animal and human excreta hidden among wild bushes on a plot of wasteland we called "mangro," short for mangrove. It was located a few hundred feet below Mama's fenced yard. There was also a huge gutter often filled with green moss and ringworms that required a huge jump to scale its width. Parents used to fuss over the occasional report that someone had fallen into that gutter. Now it is paved over, but back then it was a civil engineer's nightmare. It was supposed to channel water from Golden Grove to Perry Bay. But with the sewage water stagnant and open, the gutter created an unsanitary fiasco for the entire neighbourhood.

There were still other hazards: boys and dogs. One day, as I crossed the mangrove, I was chased all the way to the front of the house of a local tailor, Mr. Mack. I had never seen such large dogs before, as this was not my usual path to the top of the hill. Unfortunately, I found trouble on my own, walking straight into the dogs' path, due to the slight detour I took trying to avoid passing a group of boys at the corner. At school, such boys were nuisances. They were products of the C and D streams at school because they could not read well, and no one had the time or skill to teach them. They were perceived as hopeless when it came to the three R's, but were sometimes good athletes, artists and craftsmen. No one capitalized on their strengths, and many were moved year after year, from one C class to another, without learning to read. Finally, they would drop out of the system out of frustration and embarrassment. These students fought the most and were always at the headmaster's office. On the street corners, they were bullies, with no sense of purpose except to inspire fear in others. To avoid them and the dogs, I chose to run back to Mama's yard.

Mama, however, was determined. I had hoped that this would end my stint with Mr. Foster, but she said, "Walk else-way and take de food, de Lord will bless you chile," she coaxed.

One day, Mama responded to my continued request to be freed from the task. I could not understand her big-heartedness for this man who was not family.

"Kindness has no boundary, don't pick and choose who to be kind to." Nevertheless, I still detested going up Greenbay Hill to Mr. Foster's.

Collecting food for the pigs from the neighbours was an abhorrent task to me, even though I had learned by this time of the value of the pigs in my life. In return for the food, Mr. Foster sent scrapings from burnt pots littered with sparse peelings of food. I could not understand at that time how Mr. Foster's putrid mixture was of any value to the hogs, but later I realized that Mama's acceptance of his offering made him feel included. He was part of the neighbourhood, sharing and exchanging. Mama understood this, and for that reason, I had to carry the pail containing Mr. Foster's leftovers. It was a sign of respect.

CHAPTER FOURTEEN

Mama Teaches Subtle Lessons

"When you smell trouble, walk else-way"

MAMA'S PHILOSOPHY ON fighting was simple: if there was a fight, run home. If someone challenged you in the schoolyard, back down and run in another direction.

"When you smell trouble, walk else-way." I assumed not all parents were giving this instruction, for neighbourhood fights were an everyday occurrence. Mama's constant warnings would often go against my natural instinct to fight back at times. However, I was no bully, nor was I a coward: I fought three times only, most often heeding to Mama's instruction to run home.

Mr. Walter's grocery shop was located up the hill en route to Mr. Foster's house, and on Saturdays, I was sent there with a basket to buy groceries for the week. Back then, staples such as flour, sugar, oil, cornmeal, canned milk, and tomato paste were purchased weekly, while 'meat kind' was purchased daily, as many of the houses lacked electricity and therefore refrigerators.

One day, before I ascended the hill, the same group of boys I had avoided earlier was playing at the foot of the hill. As I approached the narrow road, one boy stopped, looked at me and said, "Don't pass back ya." I hadn't said a word to provoke this. I chose to ignore his silly request, thinking that by the time I had completed my business at the shop and was returning home, he and his buddies would be off to Perry Bay catching crabs or wheeling old bicycle tires further up the hill. About an hour later, I descended the narrow paved road carrying the basket laden with goods on my head. Turning the corner, I found the boys still stationed exactly where I had left them. I stopped, mindful of Mama's warnings. I thought, they aren't going to stretch themselves across the street. They are only trying to scare me. I was not going to give them the pleasure this time. I continued my descent towards them, and then noticed someone had drawn a chalk line across the road.

"Don't cross de line," he said, folding his arms high above his chest and turning his head upwards looking away from me.

Houses tightly lined both sides of the street. I either had to cross the chalk line or maneuver to the side, stumbling on rocky unfinished edges or even on steps leading to someone's front door. Mama's saying floated back in my head, "When you smell trouble, walk else-way." But that would be like walking around the globe, the voice inside declared. With the loaded basket on my head, I would have had to walk back up the hill, turn right on Loblolly Hill, pass Mr. Walter's shop, descend a steep slope, make another right at the corner by the Henry's house, scurry past Mr. Salmon's shop, dart by the public showers across from Job's house, jump the big gutter and navigate through the bushy area to Mama's yard.

T'all, t'all, the voice said again. I held on to my basket, still balanced on my head, and I stepped over the line, and continued to walk. About ten feet away, I felt a wrenching pain behind my right ear. The rock struck hard and sharp and the basket landed on the ground, scattering its contents to the nearby gutter. The gush of blood felt hot on my neck, it flowed down my back, pasting my dress to thigh until it reached the sandals on my left foot. I abandoned the basket and ran screaming to Mama.

She threw her hands in the air and cried out, "Lord, have mercy, what's de matter with you chile?"

I explained.

She checked the wound and interjected one of Grandpa's maxims: "Dem children for Joseph not under no vine or fig tree-dey run wild all day."

She knew this particular boy was always in trouble and that his mother was overwhelmed by constant complaint about his behavior.

Mama brought me to the boy's parents in the same condition. I stood behind Mama's skirt as she pointed her finger at the boy.

"Me vex you know, don't interfere wid this chile again, mark you; Daisy warn him. It hurt me bad when anybody take advantage ah this chile." Mama chided.

I looked on, smiling inside.

He got a good thrashing, plus extra for the money his mother had to reimburse Mama for the food she had lost. You knew he was accustomed to such beatings, for his face displayed little pain or embarrassment.

Later, as Mama washed the wound on my head, I grimaced from the burning sensation of the daub of iodine she applied.

Mama said, "You see why I say when you smell trouble, walk else-way?" I understood. I had gotten some satisfaction from the beating he got, yet it was no salve to the throbbing pain I felt for days at the back of my ear, or the hot tetanus injection I received with a blunted needle. But it was not easy to walk the other way if you grew up in Gray's Farm; the prospects for adventure were many and often too enticing. The smell of trouble was not always a deterrent.

CHAPTER FIFTEEN

Girls Are Different

"Don't Follow Bad Company To Do Evil."

What are little girls made of, made of?
What are little girls made of?
Sugar and spice, and everything nice,
That's what little girls are made of.
What are little boys made of, made of?
What are little boys made of?
Snips and snails, and puppy dog tails,
That's what little boys are made of.

O N THE FIRST day in kindergarten, or "infant school," I learned to recite this poem. Back then, it seemed just a funny poem and the girls giggled as we recited the first verse, and then jeered at the boys on the second. I was to learn other ways that boys and girls were different.

My cousin Fitzroy and I were eleven months apart, and back then there were rules that governed our play and pastimes as boy and girl. There were some mutual activities, such as playing marbles, a game of cricket, or even flying a kite, but he had the unfettered right to traverse outside of the yard and I did not.

Running around in King George V's pasture, swinging on the branches of flamboyant trees, swimming in Perry Bay, stoning birds in the harbor, and climbing trees in the neighboring village, were all pleasures Fitzroy enjoyed and I did not, simply because I was a girl.

One day, I asked Mama about this. She turned and said to me, "Girls stay in the yard, girls don't walk 'bout."

Mama insisted that I learn to wash, clean house, and cook meals. I did not mind these chores, because they afforded me the opportunity to be with her. Even in church, while girls were allowed to join the choir, only boys were allowed to serve at the altar. By age twelve, the demarcation between gender roles was very clear to me. I had even learned to accept most of them. Still, there was one activity that I was not allowed to do, and this I could not accept.

For some reason, I enjoyed climbing. I climbed the turtle-berry tree on the far side of Grandpa's yard, and hoped not to get caught. I climbed the old shed at the side of the house when no adults were around.

Whenever I was caught, Mama always warned, "Yuh girl, yuh too love to climb; yuh not a tomboy. Yuh going to break some part of you. Girls not supposed to climb." But there was a sweet sense of freedom I felt when I was high above the ground.

She might have had other reasons then but I knew the local superstition: if girls climbed fruit trees, the fruits would become sour. One day, when I asked Mama about this, she laughed softly and said, "That's just a way to keep girls under their mammies' watch." I was surprised that she did not play along with the local superstition by offering an ambiguous answer. Rather, she said that many of the local superstitions were handed down from generation to generation, most times without question. It was up to individuals, she said, to believe or not.

I never believed the superstition about girls climbing trees: I had eaten enough sour mangoes, plums, oranges, and tamarind from trees that had never been climbed by girls. Something else was turning fruits sour. It was not just girls.

The fact that I was not allowed to climb trees, made me want to do so even more. So when the opportunity came, I forgot every warning I had heard from Mama. Nothing could dissuade me one particular morning as I walked to school.

Fitzroy and I had just left Mama's galvanized gate on the way to Greenbay Primary School and we were about to approach Claris's Bake Shop, when a mischievous look took over his face.

"You want to hang out with me today and climb a tree?" he asked. I was taken by surprise. Fitzroy often said I was not a fun person to hang with because I bowed too quickly to Mama's interrogations. Very often I told on him whenever he left the yard for prolonged periods, if he failed to complete his chores, or whenever he took money from her hiding places. These were the moments when he would be creative with nicknames. He would call me names such as "Meme Lippy," "Mama's mouth organ" or "chatter box." Now I was happy to be back on good terms with my cousin, and to be even included in one of his escapades—scudding (skipping) school and climbing trees all day.

"Yes," I said quickly, "meet me this afternoon by Mrs. Walter's class."

Fitzroy made a sucking sound, "Fooly girl, ah mean right now, now—all marning until lunch time. Yuh coming?"

Climb trees all morning? What a prospect! What forbidden pleasure!

Fitzroy wanted an immediate answer, as we were already at the location he had in mind. But I had never missed school before except for illness or to spend a day with Mama at her job. Fitzroy on the other hand had done so before and received a good thrashing from Daddy Edmund afterwards.

Still, it seemed as if it was the kind of thing boys were expected to do, not girls. The idea of skipping school to climb trees was definitely new to me. I was a little apprehensive.

"So, what yuh going do all morning, just climb?" I asked.

"Yes. We're not going to do any of the things dey have us do in school," he replied, slowly convincing me on this point.

On a typical day, we would arrive at school by nine in the morning. We would line up military style, class by class, in front of the buildings in the quadrangle. There were some students without shoes, some without books, and some with hair uncombed. Inspection time was embarrassing to all. Though we were old enough to groom ourselves, teachers examined nails, hair, teeth and underarms for cleanliness, tidiness, and odor. Sometimes, a ruler landed on the knuckles of a child with dirty nails or he received a rough touch in the head, a taunt for uncombed hair. Some teachers came prepared to rectify such hair styles, and thought very little about the embarrassment to a boy hauled out in front of his peers, as a dirty comb was dragged through his hair. At the end of the inspection, that single comb might have groomed a half dozen heads. A boy's shirt had to be tucked into his pants, which was difficult if he was belt-less and his trousers lapped at the front into a loose knot.

Girls were not spared the humiliation. Degrading remarks about body odor, un-ironed clothes, or uncombed hair were a constant refrain. Harsh words like "worthless," " "nasty" or "use arm stick…" though directed at a few individuals, were equally felt by all.

The stress of inspection was followed by a soothing cup of hot reconstituted milk. It warmed many stomachs, many of whom had nothing to eat that morning.

Considering Fitzroy's alternative, I was filled with curiosity and excitement, but still I hesitated. I had watched the truant officer chase boys between alleys, and later cart them off to the head teacher's office for a good whipping, or to Skerritt, the juvenile detention facility. Some boys never recovered from the time spent there.

Generally, boys were the only culprits. Occasionally girls were truants, but there was no juvenile home for them, so they were never picked up.

The mischief in my cousin's eyes was irresistible. But there were other concerns: Mama's trust and my unfamiliarity with scudding (cutting class). I could take a whipping for climbing, but deceiving and disappointing Mama would be more difficult. This was not something she expected. She often said, "Don't follow bad company to do evil."

"But Mama will know," I whispered. "She'll know we didn't go to school."

"You 'fraid, gal. She can't know if you don't tell," Fitzroy replied. He had a point; this was 1967. There weren't any telephones at home, and there were none at school. Teachers could not call home to say that we were absent.

We stopped by a small bridge overlooking a place everyone called Harbor. It was not a huge patch of land, but it was big enough to be a small playground. The huge unfinished gutter ran through it, and tall coconut trees were scattered throughout the triangular-shaped space. The most striking things about Harbor were the thick foliage, the sounds of birds, and the hundreds of tiny black baby crabs that scurried on the ground. As we left the main road, the patches of green foliage seemed to wave in the morning breeze, the coconut palms seemed to nod affirmatively at me. "Yeah, let's go," I said.

There are rules when you scud school Fitzroy informed me. We couldn't be conspicuous or openly rowdy; we had to be invisible. In a small village, everyone knew everyone, and Gray's Farm Road was a major thoroughfare. So we had to keep out of the view of all adults, since adults had the authority to chastise children in any place, at any time of day.

However, Harbor was strategically placed. It was situated away from the road, and any access to the area meant one had to step down into the gutter and walk along the edge about a hundred yards from the road.

Eric Carthy's two-story variety shop also hid Harbor from direct view. We carved out our positions and set ourselves up to spend the morning away from school.

We hid among the cluster of greenery in silence, only occasionally belting out screams of euphoria. We laughed when a few adults tried to follow the trail of our sounds. But they failed, for we were well hidden by the lush foliage. For a moment my mind drifted to Mama, but I reasoned that I was already late for school; it did not make sense to abandon the plan now. The pleasure of the climbing chased Mama from my mind. Fitzroy and I swung from branches like monkeys, and watched dried leaves flutter like helicopters toward the ground. Lizards abandoned their camouflage, and scrambled out of our paths. Birds shrieked in the sky. The smell of bread from the nearby bakery filled my head, bringing to mind imagery of hot bread and butter, and igniting a sudden hunger. We slid down the trees and chased the jumbie crabs back into their holes. We climbed up again until our hands ached from the rugged tree trunks. We repeated the same activity again and again, awaiting a sign that it was time to return home. Before long, I began to feel tired and bored. Scudding was not as much fun as I had thought it would be.

After what seemed like hours, we spotted a few school children. They weren't from our school, but according to their uniforms, they attended private schools in the city. It was lunchtime, we thought. My throat was parched, my hair was frayed at the ends, my yellow gingham dress had smudges of green on it, and my forehead was burned and sweating from the sun. Fitzroy and I jumped out of the tree, brushed ourselves clean and walked towards home. Our shadows had shortened, which was another sign that it was midday: lunchtime. I dragged myself home like a lost dog as Mama's face surfaced again in my mind. Suddenly, I remembered that she was off from work for the week because it was the end of the sugar crop season. I realized that it was the worst time to be a truant.

Minutes later, we pushed open the rickety gate to the house. Fitzroy, without an iota of guilt, greeted Mama, "Good af'noon, Mama."

"Af'noon, dear Mama!" I shouted, polishing my greeting with a salve of sweetness. She pushed her head out of the window as we walked through the path between house and fence, a puzzled look on her face. We continued walking towards the back door. Mama moved quickly from the window and stood at the backdoor entrance to the house, hands on her hips, her eyes shadowed by a knitted pair of eyebrows.

Fitzroy boldly looked back at her, nothing on his face indicated guilt. He had had lots of practice with deception over the years, though he rarely outwitted her. I, on the other hand, could not even attempt to hide my sin. I have always felt that Mama could read my thoughts with those slanted eyes. She never missed the traces of salt around a forehead indicating that someone had gone to the beach without permission.

Mama examined my dress, the smudge of chlorophyll, the tear, and the leaf in my hair.

"Afternoon?" she asked. "Wha happen at school?"

Fitzroy stoically responded, "Nothing, Mama. Is lunch time. Please for lunch."

She repeated. "Please for lunch? Why you all home so early? It's not twelve yet!"

I tried to answer but my response was not audible.

Fitzroy remained steadfast, "School over, Mama."

"School over? Is only eleven, where the two of you coming from?" She said looking us over from head to toe. "Lord, look on your clothes."

I could not keep up the charade any longer. I could not continue to look her in the eye as if she could be fooled. I knew how she hated being taken for a fool. It was disrespectful, and, she always declared, where children were concerned, she was "one damn big woman" and felt insulted when perceived as not being smart enough.

She would say, "I went to school too, you know." She would recite a verse or two from Tennyson, Stevenson, or Browning, as if she had learned them just yesterday.

The whole escapade tumbled out of me while the sun squeezed cups of sweat from my forehead. "Mama, Fitzroy told me to scud school with him," I confessed. It was cowardly, but I had to try to save my own skin.

Mama replied, "He didn't knock you unconscious and drag you up the tree, did he?"

Of course she was right. I couldn't blame anyone but myself. I wasn't kidnapped, I wasn't cajoled. I had to take responsibility for my own actions.

By midday we received a good whipping, while Grandpa Cubana shouted from his side of the fence, "Hit dem hard in they head, mek dem dead. Hit dem in the ear, mek them hear."

Afterward, we were marched to school by Mama and received another whipping from the headmaster. Later, I had to stand with my arms folded in the back of the classroom and my eyes closed. It was the last time I skipped school.

Later Mama May said in the evening that she was more disappointed with me than with Fitzroy because I loved school.

"You're a girl. Yuh can't hang around like this. You're only eleven." She said bad things could happen climbing up those trees at Harbor. She didn't say the same to Fitzroy. She was angrier at me because I had chosen to follow someone to do wrong.

"Don't follow bad company to do evil," she reminded me again.

I would hear this time and time again as Mama continued to guide me and all the children in her care.

CHAPTER SIXTEEN

Mama Is Challenged

"God nawh sleep."

MAMA TOLD ME of the constant fear she had of not protecting her children enough. I wondered if most parents felt that way. I certainly felt that way, raising my children, wanting to shield them from every hurtful scenario possible. Ironically though, it was this same fear that caused Mama to disengage from our pain so that lessons could be learned when we were growing up.

She was not technically the chief disciplinarian in the house but occasionally took on the role. Her discipline, though, was of a different style than that of Daddy Edmund, who whipped us with old leather belts, coconut brooms, or packing (strips from an engine belt). Mama's reprimands usually started with a verbal warning, followed by a time lapse. During the time lapse, it was Mama's hope that we would think about our actions, the outcome and the possible consequences. If we kept up what we were doing, she went into "lock down". "Lock down" was Mama's silent treatment. It meant she had lost the will to speak to the offender.

She had another saying: "I'll give you the length of de rope, cause I know you go hang yourself." Daily, we received varying lengths of rope according to her tolerance. But once her patience was fully extended, God came to help her and we suffered.

Our disobedience to Mama's wishes was not the result of disrespect. We were simply children propelled by our environment. Gray's Farm was perfect for childhood adventures; but parents saw them as opportunities for "waywardness." Perry Bay, Side Hill beach, and Dieppe Bay called to us to swim in them. Cooks Estate, which supplied us with sugar cane and trees bursting with mangoes, tamarind, cashew, as well as cherries, invited us to climb and to feast, sometimes offering a place for a cookout. It was no wonder children stayed away from their homes or absented themselves from school. The King George V playground at the entrance of the village was lined with flamboyant trees adorned with swings and surrounded by sand pits.

So, with disobedience trailing us like a bridal train, Mama's constant pleas to "stay in the yard, don't walk about," went unheeded.

These adventures were the occasions when fights would break out, stones were thrown, and children got cuts or broken limbs. One friend lost an eye crawling under a house, another was electrocuted by an exposed street light wire. So, parents battled our spirit of adventure at every turn. When we were stubborn, they looked to God to teach us lessons. It was then that Mama declared, "God nawh sleep."

When I was eleven years old, my grandmother Annie came for her weekly Saturday visit to dote on the "children me daughter Ruth dead lef." Each time my grandmother visited, she would tell me about my mother, and swore that I looked exactly like her:

"You de pittance ah Ruth," she would say to me.

After a proper inspection and other preliminaries, Grandmother would unload limes and tea bush into my hands from Parham, or fruits and tasty cakes she had bought at the St. John's Market. Mama had become impatient with the selfish manner in which I received these gifts and instructed that the packages be placed on the table to be shared with the other children in the house.

Predictably, I was not thrilled about this, preferring to share at my own whim and fancy. I ignored Mama's directive. After all, it was my parcel, and my grandmother, I silently insisted.

On this particular visit, my grandmother placed a small pumpkin in my hand, an unusual gift. Mama gave me a stern look, but I quickly turned away. A few minutes later, Mama exited the gate to visit a neighbour, but not before issuing a final warning:

"Monica," she said, "put de pumpkin with de other food provisions on de table. Ah making soup for Sunday dinner."

I wanted to cut open that pumpkin to see the burst of colours on the inside. Minutes later, I had my opportunity when my grandmother left to visit my sister Eunette, who at the time was living with Mama's mother, Pepsi. Grabbing the nearest knife, one whose blade was chipped as an old comb, I sat on a box and rested the pumpkin on my right knee. I slowly began a sawing motion. It took some pressure, but eventually the knife zigzagged its way through the gourd.

The blood did not appear instantly when the jagged knife tore open my knee. At first only tiny spots of blood oozed in. I cried out for Mama. She rushed frantically back to the yard, calmly picked up the shattered pumpkin, and walked over to where I stood a few feet away. My screams stopped for a moment, for her presence was always a comfort. However, she remained transfixed and stepped away without touching me.

"God nawh sleep," I heard her say. "Monica what did I say before I walk out the gate? How many times I warn your grandmother?" A note of triumph pinching her words.

I felt alone, unloved, and abandoned. She had often come to my aid. At the house, small fights with cousins were broken up or won in my favor, because Mama was in my corner. Now, teaching me a lesson was more important than showing the love I knew she had for me. As my grandmother reappeared to bandage the wound, Mama pouted and hummed, but I swore she winced from my cries of pain, as iodine was put on.

At times of leisurely reflection, Mama would remind me of how "funny" she was towards disobedience. To reinforce her point, she reminded me of an incident involving her grandson, Byron.

She sent Byron to the standpipe for water. Even though he was long overdue in returning with the water, she waited, giving him "the length of a rope." Finally, pouting and in "lock down" mode, she walked to the standpipe to find him. Byron was nowhere in sight. Mama filled the abandoned bucket, knowing that her alliance with God would avenge Byron's disobedience.

An hour later, Byron came in the gate screaming at the top of his lungs. One side of his shin was badly cut and bruise. He also had a large gash below his elbow. Mama did not ask about his whereabouts, but he volunteered the information.

Byron explained, "Mama, my friend know I can't ride bike and he still give me a ride."

"Here he comes, selling at nine eggs a penny," were her exact words. It was her idiom for when someone's story didn't pan out or when the reasoning made no sense.

Byron's injury was serious enough to need medical attention, so Mama changed her clothes in order to take Byron to the hospital. Just then, a neighbour came into the yard and reported that Byron had actually been hurt down at Side Hill Bay. Angry, Mama changed back into her home clothes and went about her chores.

"God nawh sleep," was all she said. Byron was a much-loved grandson, but the lesson had to be learned. She had warned him just days before about the same bike: now the "length of rope" had twisted around Byron's neck and the bad bruise and cut were the result. His disobedience made her angry. Angry enough to change from the "town clothes" she had donned, and to her "home clothes."

Mama ignored Byron's tears and prepared dinner. Her lips were set in their familiar pout, her shoulders curved. Being quite a few years older than Byron, and seasoned to Mama's attitude towards disobedience, I wrapped his wound with a cloth and accompanied him to the hospital myself, where he received seven stitches.

Over the years, I grew to understand Mama's attitude toward such transgressions. Mama would fill in some of the gaps about past examples of our disobedience growing up. There was for instance, the story of Ira, her teenage son.

One day a neighbour reported that Ira was once again at Perry Bay, perched on an abandoned iron barge. Perry Bay was the closest of all the bays in that section of Antigua. It was an integral part of village life back then. It was where children frolicked and poked fun at blowfish called toady. We splattered the gelatinous remains of jellyfish on the sand. It was where, after the tides receded, we dug for baby clams called dice, which made a tasty seasoned rice dish. Fishermen hauled in nets, while children clamored for the unwanted crayfish and smaller fish. Women would meet in the early mornings to dispose of excreta accumulated in enamel pails.

Perry Bay did have the occasional drowning, which was part of Mama's worries. We were duly warned, "Don't go bayside without me, or you all go drown."

Mama's sons knew she could not swim, so they enjoyed a laugh behind her back and disobeyed her. A mother who never learned to swim was not unusual, even in my time. Most girls simply did not have the privilege of straying from the yard, or the watchful eyes of their mothers to spend hours at the beach. The boys had no such restraint. As a result, they were great swimmers. For disobeying Mama's orders, her sons faced whippings and extra chores once Mama had examined necklines for sand, or used her tongue to taste for salt residue on foreheads. Of course, the boys would wash away any telltale signs at the public standpipe, or would shower at the public bathroom on Parliament Street, once they learned Mama's strategy.

Once Mama absorbed the news of Ira being down at the bay, she quickly tied her head with a red cloth, pushed her feet into a pair of old yard shoes, and breathlessly hurried up Gray's Farm Road. She turned the corner at Mrs. Martin's bread shop, and shuffled past Christian's Ironworks. Mama raced through Tinning Village to the seashore. The raw smell of the ocean filled Mama's nostrils as fear of the sea curled her spine and caused her to shiver.

She spied Ira about a hundred yards away, perched on the old sea vessel, and beckoned him to come ashore. Ira looked back at her, filled with fear and disbelief that Mama was actually there. He knew he was hanging at the length of Mama's rope because it had only been a week ago that she had questioned him about this barge, and he had emphatically denied ever being near it.

"Miss May, de boy fu you out in de seawater," someone had said.

Instead of trusting fate, hoping for lenience, and swimming straight into Mama's grasp, Ira jumped sideways from the barge and into the sky blue water. His plan was to come ashore a small distance from where she stood.

He felt the pain instantly. A piece of rusted metal from a wrecked vessel had pierced his kneecap. When he came ashore, his face was contorted with pain.

Mama stood paralyzed. Her heart pounding in her chest as if it were knocking desperately, trying to get out. A buried memory rose from the caverns of her mind. She swallowed hard and pushed it back.

"God nawh sleep," she muttered.

Deep inside, Mama felt the pain, but she had given Ira the length of a rope, and now he had to suffer the consequences. This must be his last perch on that barge, she promised silently.

That night both Ira and Mama lost sleep as he tossed and cried out. A few nights later, Mama applied warm cloths to the wound and gave him Phensic, an aspirin, for his pain. As he suffered day and night with the pain, Mama did, too. Repeated flashes of his body leaping sideways into the water interrupted her thoughts. She was gripped by fear and by facing the reality that Ira could have drowned. She imagined the struggle: his head surfacing one, two, three times, before slowly slipping under the water. If Ira had not been a strong swimmer, Mama would not have been able to save him, and that made her scared and angry enough to let him suffer some more.

Several days later, he developed a fever and Mama promptly took him to the doctor's office located near the Country Pond in town. Mama left the room nauseated, as Ira screamed her name. She wept secretly in the hallway as blood, inflammation, and water were suctioned out of his knee. She knew Grandie Sophie would have handled this in a different way. But Ira had pushed her to the limit. Mama realized that because of her inability to swim and her fear of the sea, she might have had to watch a child die for the second time in her life.

One day in 1953, Mama went to work and left her son Barrymore, who was three years old, in the care of her son Ira. That morning, Ira went to pick mangoes on Kentish Road and took the toddler with him. While Ira climbed and played with friends, Barrymore ate tiny mangoes one after the other. The mangoes, though barely past the nascent stage, had dropped to the ground, littering the shaded area beneath the mother tree. No one could explain why Barrymore found the young mangoes palatable, as they were never edible due to their strong acidity, but he ate his belly full. It was many hours before Mama returned from work to discover her sick child.

Back then, folks sought out doctors with great reluctance and only after exhausting home-remedy options.

"Is just a lickle bellyache," "Nah worry," "Give de chile some home-remedy," were the usual responses.

Mama May, thirty-three years old at the time, was caught on a wheel spun by tradition and respect.

Someone said, "Rub de chile nable with lamp oil."

Another neighbour said, "Put a few drops ah Angostura bitters in water."

Grandpa was the one who prevailed: "Go buy de senna leaf. Dat will work de belly."

Filled with fear and surrounded by confusion, Mama brewed a potent cup of the dried senna leaves and coaxed Barrymore to drink it. That night, the child lay in bed alongside his older sister, Elaine.

Everyone in the household listened helplessly as the child constantly cried, "Me belly! Me belly!"

The pungency of embryonic mangoes and the harsh action of senna trapped in the delicate stomach and intestines of a small child proved deadly. Mama's tears, tremors, or balls of sweat around her forehead could not save her child that night. As the hours dragged on, the child's liver became damaged. Barrymore died before the morning sun could eat the dew over Perry Bay.

Mama felt she had not done enough and vowed to God that it would not happen again. Ira's jump into the sea had caused Mama to revisit buried memories of ignorance, incompetence, and guilt.

"Lord have mercy, look you could've drown right in front of me," she had said to Ira. "God nawh sleep."

But it was not just a warning or recognition of pain. To Mama, the expression was a celebration, and a comfort, because she believed that God's constant vigilance kept Ira from sinking to the bottom of Perry Bay.

On other occasions, when I would see the frustration on her face as she fussed with or whipped a son or grandson who had disobeyed her, I could not understand why she cried sometimes. I came to realize, however, that our disobedience was a sort of punishment for Mama too, for she was pained every time we were hurt. Perhaps she realized that her desire to protect us could not be successful without some degree of cooperation on our part. However, when challenged by our willful spirits, Mama held on to the surety that God really was not asleep.

CHAPTER SEVENTEEN

Tragedy In Mama's Life

"Don't worry, things will work out."

IT STARTED IN 1968. I was not yet thirteen; my brother Eardley was twenty one years old. He had joined Mama's household back in 1959, when our father died. Due to Mama's insistence that everyone "learn a skill, and do sub'm useful," Eardley became a skilled carpenter.

One day, as he leaned out of a window, he stopped me on my way out of the gate. He wanted me to run to the store for him. When he made his request, I couldn't help but notice that his eyes were not focused on me. Eardley's focus was off and that gave me a weird feeling. He had been complaining about headaches lately, which must have been very bad, because he was never one to complain. He kept to himself, was quiet and very shy. I remember Mama insisting that Daddy Edmund accompany Eardley on his next visit to the doctor.

I waited anxiously for Mama to return from work that afternoon.

"Mama, Eardley is going blind," I said.

"Why you think so?" she queried

"Mama, he was looking down at me from the window in the front of the house, and his eyes focused way past me as he spoke."

In the next few weeks as a result of Mama's connections with the ruling political party, Eardley was on a plane to Jamaica for surgery. He was diagnosed with brain cancer, and given six months to live. He returned to Antigua to Mama's care and a painful death.

I had no tears left in me at Eardley's funeral. For months when he lived, I helped Mama tend to him. I cried alone at night, at school and in church.

This was a difficult time in Mama's household. Months before, Daddy Edmund had gone off to marry another woman. Mama was busy working, and keeping the family together. The young ones in the house were insensitive to suffering, death and loss. Mama held us all together somehow, as we buried, mourned, and grieved in our own ways for the loss of one of the children God had placed into her care. Who would know more deaths were to follow in just a few years time?

From the early part of 1974, I watched Mama console her son Jerome. He seemed too old to be consoled by a mother, as he was already married with children. He lived in Hatton Estate, which was a mile or so west of Gray's Farm Village. But Mama's house was where he came for love, consolation, explanation, affirmation, or whatever his soul needed. He would generally appear in the afternoons after she was home from work. Usually, he would find her seated over a coal pot, the night's dinner bubbling as she fanned the flames to accelerate the cooking. He knew she would always find the time to listen, even when she was busy. In his usual stooped stance, Jerome would lean across from his mother talking about his concerns.

"Don't cry, son, things will work out," she would say.

At nineteen years old, I was still considered too young to be involved in adult business, so I just watched and listened silently. But I knew that my cousin was troubled and pained.

In Antigua then, physical illness was the only acknowledged sickness. If Jerome needed psychiatric help, as concerned as Mama was, neither she, nor anyone else would have known what to do. If his hands were not bleeding, his limbs were not broken, or if he did not have fever or vomiting, then, according to conventional wisdom, he should be able to fix himself. Some even thought he was malingering.

"You can behave better."

"Forget about it, jack."

"Snap out of it."

"Try to move on."

These were all typical responses.

To me, Jerome evoked memories of my father— of a man slowly losing everything. His marriage was falling apart and he was concerned about his children. Imagine, a man concerned about his children! This again was Mama's influence, as Jerome too, had heard her say, "babies come from heaven, tek care ah dem." None of us could operate contrary to this powerful message, which had been passed down from Sophie. Even today, none of Mama's male children have ever abandoned their offspring. Pomroy, Ira, Fitzroy and Barrymore, raised their children for many years with the absence of mothers.

Jerome couldn't understand the instruction to "move on." For him, to live away from his family meant that his children would suffer.

My cousin was a handsome man. He was a talented cricketer, an excellent welder, and an artist who painted beautiful landscapes. As a teenager, I looked forward to seeing him. For those minutes that sometimes turned into hours, Mama would offer him food, listened to whatever he had to say, and give him advice. However, Jerome was changing with every visit.

As in Dostoevsky's *The Double*, Jerome moved and acted like two persons. There were days when he was calm, and lucid. As an avid reader, there were times when he walked into the yard with a novel in his hand. However, there were other days when his speech was incoherent, his eyes too penetrating, and his laughter misplaced. These were days when his head hung in Mama's lap like a child. He seemed then like a man who had been beaten by his own manhood.

As Mama observed her son, she may have questioned what she had done over the years for him to display such unmanly behaviour. Daddy Edmund and Grandpa had never displayed their feelings openly.

"Don't cry," I often heard her say to Jerome, "Things will work out. The children will understand." However, it did not matter, because Jerome did not understand. He did not understand that if he were not alive, his children would have to grow up without him. He could not understand, because the troubled and depressed do not function in such a manner. He only felt that his nerves wanted respite. He had been troubled and depressed for months, and now the symptoms manifested themselves in this split between his real self and his "double." I suspect this was another time when Mama felt that her hands were tied, for how could she force a grown man to go to doctor? Why did he need one anyway? Mental illness in a small village would bring on a family shame that would never be forgotten. This was her son.

I had seen the signs. We'd all seen the signs.

A shower of sadness drenched the household one early morning when the news came to Mama that Jerome was taken to hospital; he tried to commit suicide. For the next week, I watched Mama return from hospital in the mornings, every time with a pair of pajamas and towels to be washed. She tenderly held on to the soiled garments, washing, rinsing, ironing, and folding them as if doing his laundry would keep him alive. Then she walked the hill in the evenings to hospital to see him, to wipe his face, to talk, to pray and to hope.

I visited Jerome only once for that was all I could take. There was little response from him then, for the substance he had taken was slowly shutting down his liver and kidneys. I suspected Jerome was struggling to stay alive because he saw Mama's pain. A few days later, Jerome died. Mama had no more pajamas and towels to launder.

His double had won. It had convinced him that life was no longer worth the stress, the heartbreak, the disappointments, the deception, and the fragmentation of his family. Jerome took his life and left Mama and the rest of the family in deep pain, guilt, and shame. It was unfortunate that he had fallen sick on an island that did not acknowledge mental illness. In the end, Jerome had been unable to "snap out of it and move on." What were his last thoughts before he drank that substance, I often wondered? What faces flashed before his eyes as the liquid took its effects? His father? His children? Other family members? Mama?

A deep sound thundered from the bottom of Mama's gut, which reminded me of my father's funeral fifteen years before. Perhaps it came from the same place Uncle Pomroy had screamed from, back in 1959.

"Don't worry Mama," I said. "I am here for you."

I wanted to take her away from the pain. I wanted to brush her dress off, and I wanted to believe again, for her sake, that Jerome would get out of that box, and walk away from all the bad, singing and crying. But, I was no longer four years old.

Mama seemed as if she was drowning in the loss of her son. Her well-defined pout was now firmly in place. As the days, weeks, and months passed, she held her head high, for she had known tragedies over the years. Jerome was the fourth child she had to bury, and she hoped there would be no more. Grandie Sophie, Pepsi, and Uncle Brother had died in old age and she had cared for them to the end. Parents expected children would be left to bury and grieve after they were gone, not the reverse. Mama spoke to God at night and in church. She turned the grief inwards and pounds melted from her body.

Six months later, Mama was at a gravesite to bury another child. This time, it was thirty-eight-year-old Rhonie, who died in St. Thomas after giving birth. Mama, it seemed, had one last sound from that same place in her belly. It did not sound as deep and distinct as it had at Jerome's funeral. She held her belly instead of her chest because that was the place where deep loss and grief were felt.

Days before Mama left for St. Thomas, a murmuring sound took over her; her head would shake and I would hear a sound like that of a wounded animal. Her jaws displayed the familiar pout and Mama's eyes looked out as if she were seeing nothing. She had just been to that place with Jerome, now there was nothing left for Rhonie but long muffled groans, which replaced cries and tears.

I watched Mama pack a small suitcase and leave for St. Thomas the very next day. I was left in charge of the household and her affairs. She buried Rhonie in St. Thomas; there would be no graveside visits. One-week-old Junior Hazelwood, Rhonie's child, extended the list of children God placed in Mama's care.

Junior adjusted quickly to life without his mother, but for Mama, the adjustments were not as easy. But drawing on the energy of her ancestors – especially on her grandmother Sophie—Mama found the tenacity to endure the grief. She asked God to end the loss of her children.

"No more," she said, "Lord, no more!"

She now had to raise a grandchild who had lost his mother hours after birth. Mama also had to nurture the other grandchildren. She had to have the strength to comfort neighbours or protect those who needed her as shield during a spousal fight. Grandpa was still alive then, and he needed her as the sounding board for his eccentricities and verbal abuse. We, in the immediate household needed her, too. Fitzroy and I added our rebellious nature to the mix. Jerome had left behind five children who were pained with the loss – Byron, Mervin, Linda, Junior, and Ian. Mama, through all this, fought the grief at night after days of working at the Fiennes Institute caring for the destitute, to whom she also had to offer love and comfort.

With so many young children in Mama's care, visits to the pediatric clinic kept her busy, now at the age of fifty-five. Mumps, diphtheria and polio once again became concerns. Washing Birdseye diapers and making cornmeal and barley porridges added another level of commitment. Through it all, Mama ploughed ahead.

"Things will work out," she said.

In rare moments of despondency, she would remark, "God don't give you more than you can bare."

In the face of her children's deaths, Mama reveled in the births of a few new grandchildren in 1975. That same year provided highlights such as my marriage, the birth of my daughter Monifa, my admission to Teacher's College, and Mama's first trip to America. She also continued an active social life in politics and trade unionism, and caring for her extended family. I was amazed at how Mama embraced life and moved on.

CHAPTER EIGHTEEN

Good Grooming

"Be Presentable Every Time You Leave De House."

"**B**E PRESENTABLE EVERY time you leave de house," Mama often said. Just as she would say, "always mek up yuh bed; yuh never know if yuh have to come back sick." These were drilled into my psyche over the years.

Sometime during the course of my journey with Mama, dressing her for special occasions became my job. I could not recall exactly when it started but it never ended, even after I had left her house as an adult. There were even the occasional times, over the years when I returned from my adopted home of New York and assisted her. Thankfully, this was not because of any inability on her part to perform this task, but because of her desire to revisit memories as we bonded during this ritual.

It was as if one day, sometime the late '60's, that Mama had decided that her personal grooming—hair washing and drying, bathing, toe and fingernail clipping, ear cleaning, and anointing aching muscles—were no longer things with which she should be burdened. They were now my responsibility.

By the time I was fourteen years old, I had become more involved in her personal upkeep, which drew us together, like two peas in a pod. My muscles ached from scrubbing Mama's knees repeatedly. I scrubbed her heels with a rough stone and gently lifted and washed her large breasts, which rested lazily on her high abdomen. As I look back now, that transition seemed automatic. There'd been no discussion about it, no persuading or pleading.

We had no indoor plumbing at that time. Everyone had a white enamel pail or commode, known locally as a tensile or *poe*, which was used as a toilet at night. Every morning, I emptied the collected urine at the far end of the backyard, over the roots of a healthy privy tree.

I also provided Mama with a good rub, which was the panacea to the "old pains" in Mama's knees and lower back. I learned the list of remedies from her: Canadian healing oil, Iodex, Radiant B, and mustard cream. Adding to the ointments were the local superstitions. Mama believed that rubbing with the left-hand rid her muscles of aches and pains. I rubbed the aching body part, transferring Mama's pain by tapping on a nearby wooden object within arm's reach. It was then that the belching commenced. The sounds came almost like thunder with every compression to particular areas around the ribs and upper back.

There was some gratification for me, as she intoned, "God bless you, chile. How they say you going be ungrateful—that you will bite off me ear? But look you here to do all this for Mama. The Lord bless you."

Those phrases meant a great deal to me. I felt that Mama was bestowing on me, God's fortunes for the future. These were the moments of vindication and affirmation. There was reciprocity of love from her. These were the moments when no one else in the world mattered except Mama and me.

Like a colony of ants, we lived, smelled, and fed on each other. There was an exclusive female bond that tied us together as we scurried back and forth in our roles in each other's lives.

I had always slept in Mama's bed. It was her way of separating the sexes and shielding me from the boisterous behaviour of the boys. Looking back, I realize there was always a cloak of protection around me. Most often it operated in silence, or with the utterance of a few words or phrases like "You are a little girl, stay here with Mama."

I doubt, that every household enjoyed the dressing ritual over which Mama and I bonded. On special occasions and Sundays, Mama had to be meticulously dressed. As her lady-in-waiting, this task was mine. On any of those special Sundays, Mama's underwear were strewn across the bed: a long-line bra, slightly yellowed at the underarms, a long-legged girdle with as many hooks and eyes as a spider had legs, a half-petticoat with a border of lace, a pair of stockings, and a white handkerchief starched, ironed, and folded. Since most of Mama's dresses were tapered at the waist and flared with pleats or gathers, there was one feature on her body that was always a formidable challenge to such styles: her protruding belly. It was the main obstruction to anything she wore. My job was to camouflage this bulbous feature, using a series of tucks, tufts, heaves, huffs, and puffs, until she was finally ready.

This was how it all began. After a bath, she'd sit on a chair, just as she did when she was cooking. Every piece of every garment had to be handed to her. First, I had to fit Mama's brassiere. The body-line bra had to be connected by the hooks and eyes to encase her in an elastic shield. Though I was, by this time, taller than her five feet two inches, there was a handmade wooden box to give me the necessary elevation to complete this task. Usually, my hands sweated profusely and this brought the blood rushing toward my fingers. Mama would hold her breath and I would count "one... two... three," as I stretched to connect each pair of hook to its corresponding eye.

The next piece of garment was the girdle, the most daunting of all. It had to clear an obstacle course, which included a pair of cellulite-thickened thighs, an enormous backside, and a prominent belly. I never measured the time it took to put the girdle on, but we sweated together like wrestlers, as we gripped, tugged, and heaved to the final round. It was at that time that I lifted Mama a few inches off the floor from sheer determination.

We laughed together in those moments. "Me dear, you sorbice," Mama would say, out of breath, an affirmation of my usefulness.

"Chile, yuh have some strong muscle, yuh hear? Look how you lift Mama off the floor? The Lord bless you. Ah don't know what Mama do without you."

I stood glowing with pride.

"They say yuh going be ungrateful, but who else here now to help poor Mama?" she said, puffing and laughing, beads of sweat settling permanently around her hairline and nose. After a sweet, cooing laughter she instructed, "Chile pass the stockings."

The ordeal was far from over, for she was now unable to bend over to put on her stockings and shoes. At this point, Mama was only able to sit upright, slanting slightly backwards. Her short, stocky legs stuck out like crooked poles, her toes pointing in diverging directions. Rolling each stocking around her toes, I stopped abruptly above the knees, proceeding to connect garter straps from the girdle to the stockings.

Like a pair of masons layering bricks, we pinned them together. Mama— the structure— was now complete. Fully armored from neck to toes, she looked like an Egyptian mummy. Minutes later, I maneuvered a shoehorn around her heels as her heavy feet slipped into place.

The dress was then thrown over her head and zipped. Subsequently she was accessorized with a broad hat, earrings, and a pearl necklace. Mama was transformed. Mopping her face with a daub of white powder, she smeared some Vaseline on her thin lips. The twisting and twirling were next, and my eyes sparkled with wonder as if an imaginary halo surrounded Mama.

The Queen was now dressed and ready to go. This was one of the many times I could feel a mutual love flowing between us, and promised that I would dress myself with the same meticulous care in the future—but without the girdle!

Sunday was not only for churchgoing. Mama was also very active in the Women's Auxiliary branch of the Antigua Labor Party. A few times a year, the Auxiliary held singing competitions between sections. I boarded buses with other women, Mrs. Bailey or Mrs. Piggott at the helm, and sat at the front of the audience beaming as Mama belted out her alto against her armor of elastic lingerie. Her chest and belly would compete for elevation and I used to admire the oval shape she made with her mouth.

Easter Sunday in Mama's house meant new dresses, pants, shirts, hats, shoes, socks, and bags. Everyone in the house had new clothes. The night before, she and I would spend two hours at Mrs. Mason's or Mrs. Richards's while last minute adjustments were made to dresses. Earlier in the day, we would stop at Bata's shoe store for new shoes and at Moore's Variety Store for matching hats.

I never liked Mama's choice of hats for me back then, and she never agreed with my choice either.

"Ms. Moore, pass that white hat on the left," Mama said on this particular Saturday morning. I was bent on making my own selection. The saleswoman reached for the white hat from the glass case. The clustered store buzzed with voices; everybody was buying hats. Mama rested the hat over the plastic that was provided to protect the inside. The hat was downright ugly. It had a small circular crown that flared into a wide rim. This is not the type of hat a thirteen-year-old wears, I thought.

"Mama, I don't like that one," I said. She didn't fuss. Most parents would have said, *yuh think you big woman, you working for your own money?*

"Ms. Moore, pass that other one," she said, calmly. Meanwhile, I thought, let me choose my own hat. I'm old enough. But another year would pass before I gained such a privilege.

One Sunday, Mama announced that we were to take a family photograph. Those were the days when the photographer made house calls. Today, having a photographer come to the house to take the picture suggests some degree of affluence, but back then it simply meant that Mama had "cut and contrived," prioritized, and with resourcefulness, was able to squeeze a few dollars for a family picture. I was about eight years old. Most of Mama's children were still at home, except Pomroy. By that afternoon, we were all dressed in our "Sunday best" awaiting Mr. Warwick, the local photographer. We all gathered in the front of the house and posed for pictures, as Mama sat, queen-like, in the center, holding a younger grandchild while the rest of us surrounded her. There was a proud look on her face as some of the neighbours looked on, for such an event was a rarity in Gray's Farm.

I can still recall every moment during that picture-taking session because I had practiced an exaggerated smile all day.

"Be yuh natural self," Mama instructed. But, inevitably, as the camera flashed, I was grinning from ear to ear.

CHAPTER NINETEEN

Against Abuse

"A Coward Man Fight A Woman"

"**G**o in you house, Josephine. It takes two to make a quarrel!" Mama would caution a neighbour.

Growing up in Gray's Farm, conflicts between adults were part of the daily spectacle. The frequent verbal confrontations, what we called *cussing*, became entertainment for onlookers. Women quarrelled with one another over simple matters such as a disagreement between their children or a piece of gossip overheard.

Worse than the cussing though, were the physical fights. I was sensible enough to know that this abominable behaviour between adults was wrong. It was not a part of Mama May's household and she condemned it.

Men fought frequently with their women. These altercations routinely spilled into the streets and alleyways. I saw women with swollen faces, bloodied mouths, and open gashes on their heads.

Physical abuse was something Mama hated with a passion. The men knew this, and the women were embarrassed when Mama had to witness it. Mama shielded the women running to her door with her short stocky body, and she rebuked the men.

"George, is a coward man fight a woman." Mama's expression of disgust and disdain sometimes embarrassed the men into backing down. But occasionally she had to be more threatening.

"You damn coward, why you don't pick fight with a man, so he can buss in yuh napper case," she'd say. The last two words were never comprehensible, but their intention was clear to all. As she cursed angrily, the men walked back to their small houses, chests still high with pride and mannish victory.

The occasional police presence was never a threat as spousal abuse simply received a silent nod. Women were told to return to their houses and "behave" themselves.

Many years later, I was able to understand why she had shown such contempt for the frequent abuse the women in the neighbourhood tolerated. She had taken a stance against abuse in her early twenties. Daddy Edmund had hit her on two occasions. He was also very verbally abusive. To her, the verbal abuse was just as painful and sometimes worse, for words stayed in the memory and the pain of them lingered longer than physical abuse. With that and the other time he had hit her, Mama predicted that such behaviour would only follow them into marriage. When Daddy Edmund asked Mama to accompany him to the jeweler's so that her finger could be measured for a ring, she refused.

Marriage was seen as an honour, conferring status and a level of social respect. Happiness and respect were not guaranteed, however. Many men openly set up secondary families nearby, so that it was an accepted norm to see a man's children by different mothers playing with one another. But Mama was not the type to place a ring over her own dignity and value. She knew well how the women before her had fought against degradation from slave masters, society, and the men in their lives. The way she saw it, rejecting marriage kept her in control of her life. When Daddy Edmund left her after having eight children and married someone else, the tears were for the hurt she saw in her children, particular Barrymore who was the youngest.

Mama watched in pain as some of her neighbours dealt physically and verbally with abuse. When Mrs. Brooks came to

Mama with a broken jaw, Mama was angry. The story was that Mrs. Brooks went to the market where her husband sold fish, to "make conduct" about his mistress. Mr. Brooks then struck her in the jaw with a four-pound weight. While everyone saw the act as severe, they had grown accustomed to the volatile nature of the marriage. They were more astonished that Mrs. Brooks had left the market and walked in the opposite direction from the hospital to Gray's Farm Road just to complain to Mama.

"Mrs. Brooks, let me follow you to hospital," Mama offered, adding, "Is a coward man fight a woman. Yuh husband should be shame ah he self."

As adults fought, children fought too. Though parents warned and threatened us with beatings, they made no connection between their own behavior, and our childish mimicry. So we fought at the standpipe, in the schoolyard, after Sunday school, and at the end of confirmation classes. Stones were the weapon of choice we used to test accuracy and precision. We stoned each other and followed up with visits to the health clinic, bawling over the open cuts to the head.

Given Mama's injunction against fighting, "If someone show you fight, put you two foot in your hand and run home," I was often running in the opposite direction due the bullying nature of many children. But while children fought and then quickly mended relationships, some adults kept the enmity for long periods of time, sometimes years.

CHAPTER TWENTY

Passing the time

"Learn to cut and contrive"

I N THE SIXTIES and seventies, every house on the street had a meeting place where the adults would take turns convening. Mama's meeting place was at a large flat stone in front of Grandpa's house. With limited streetlights in the village, it was kerosene, not electricity that illuminated most of the houses. The surroundings were pitch black.

Neighbours talked and laughed long into the night over food and discussions of politics. There was no television to help pass the time, so children played games like "Bam, Bam, Bee-dee Bee-dee," or card games like "whappee" or "pat." We told riddles about fruits and vegetables, or guessed the amounts of roasted corn in the palm of another's hand.

The visiting neighbours were kept entertained not only with jokes from Mama's work, but also with stories about spirits and ghosts, beings we called *jumbies*. I used to snuggle close to Mama, terrified by the characters in the stories. Most children were reluctant to even move when the adults decided they should go to bed. Some of the stories were about my dead parents, with information added depending on the imagination of the storyteller and decisions about how much I should be teased.

Over and over I heard about Aunt Toonkoo, the eccentric ant-like old lady who lived in the house to the left side of Mama's land. When I was barely two years old, she repeatedly heard me chuckling as if someone was playing with me. Aunt Toonkoo looked over her fence and saw my mother, who had by then been dead for six months. According to Aunt Toonkoo, my mother was playing with me as I sat on an old sheet in front of Mama's house. Of course, this was Aunt Toonkoo's type of business, and she threatened my mother's spirit.

"Ruth, leave de chile alone, yuh warnt hurt her?"

"Ah just saying how Miss May caring she jack." This was what Aunt Toonkoo claimed my mother replied.

"Well you carnt play with Monica, so nawh come back round yah, or ah bottle yuh up," Aunt Toonkoo warned.

The island people's superstitions included the thinking that some people had a special gift to see *jumbies* and communicate with them. There was the occasional talk that someone had "set jumbie on" so and so. Growing up in those days, there was much fear and talk about *jumbies*, which made children afraid and confused. I returned from funerals afraid that the spirits of the dead had returned to the house and hidden under the bed or in some corner. I used to forego passing urine at night for fear of going outside in the dark.

Regretfully, that fear stayed with me way into adulthood, though Mama tried to assure me, "The dead can't harm you; be afraid of the living."

Ghosts and spirits were not the only hot topics in the village, however. Neighbours also talked about the politics, which were mainly favorable discussions about Chief Minister and later Premier, Vere Cornwall Bird Sr. Mama was an active member of Antigua Trades and Labor Union and its political arm, the Antigua Labor Party. She paid her dues religiously and attended meetings and weekly events. Most of Mama's friends were in political alliance with the ALP and AT&LU. Even the colours she wore conformed to the party she supported. She had many red dresses, and mine were often cut from the same cloth. I used to accompany her to political meetings and was even a member of the youth division of the ruling political party. I was surprised that a few times Mama boarded a small boat to attend the Labour Day celebration held at the historical Fort James, despite her fear of the sea and not being able to swim.

With a house of children to attend to, it was a marvel that Mama found time for the active social life that she led. Singing contests with Mama's women's auxiliary group took us all over the island. I attended conventions in villages such as Old Road, All Saints, and Cedar Grove, and listened to young upcoming politicians. The most notable was the young Baldwin Spencer, who has since become the Prime Minister. The adults admired his ability to speak on issues, and especially his fervent support and passionate belief in workers' rights and trade unionism.

In Gray's Farm, neighbours looked out for each other and shared anything just because someone asked. They traded eggs for a piece of cake, ice for a bottle of ginger beer, and borrowed a little flour, sugar, or salt here and there. Sometimes a villager need not even start her own coal fire to cook dinner.

"Tell Chrissie send piece ah fire." Mama would say.

Neighbours visited each other and returned home in triumph. "Walk fool better than sit down fool," Mama chuckled after many such visits. In her hands were fruits, vegetables or slabs of corned meat, or corned fish. She always cautioned, "...carry a bag with you. De neighbour can't say, well if you had a bag, I'd give you a few mangoes, few sweet potatoes or piece ah pumpkin, or so and so."

Mama herself grew spinach, squash, and peas on the fences surrounding the house. Most yards produced a few okras, cassia, papaya, or some other trees, the fruit from which supplemented meals.

Besides the bits of ingredients brought home from Mama's job, another source of food was the barrels sent by children living overseas. In addition, Daddy Edmund would bring home extra ground provisions from the plots of land he cultivated at Friar's Hill and at Briggins. Mama's sister Ruth, who had become a baker, would send bread. And of course one of the pigs under the shed had the misfortune to become dinner for a few nights.

We purchased goods and supplies from neighbourhood shops like Sammon, Mr. Parker, Mr. De Silva (Bamboo Shop), Mrs. Walters, and John on Christian Street. At that time, one could purchase cheese, butter, ham roll, and cooking butter by the ounce, rice, flour, sugar, or cornmeal by the pound or half-pound, cooking oil and kerosene oil by the half-pint, a single cigarette or needle, or an airmail envelope or sheet of writing paper.

On a daily basis, Mama would ask, "What we cooking today?" After checking the food safe, I would go to the nearest shop to purchase perishables depending on what we decided on for the night's dinner.

At the shop, credit or *trust* was based on honour: the shopkeeper would record what was taken in a large book, and payment was expected at the end of the week. One shopkeeper must have had too many delinquent and undependable customers, because one day, a sign was hung in full view: "BUY TODAY AND CREDIT TOMORROW."

Some neighbours owned cows, and would sell milk and collect "milk money" at the end of the week. Bottles of milk, flavored with fever grass or nunu balsam leaves and brown sugar, warmed my stomach most nights.

Like her neighbours, Mama watched and stretched every penny; buying staples in bulk was economical. By the time I hit fourteen years old, she would place a small, brown envelope on the table each week. It contained her wages, and we would plan how to provide for the household needs in the week ahead. On Saturdays, I went to the shops looking for bargains. Sometimes, I shopped at three stores before returning to Mama, proud that I had been able to purchase all the items on the list.

On one of those weekly visits to David Torrey's Store on Market Street, I had my customary allowance for shopping. I waited my turn and received my packages of sugar, flour, corn meal, tomato paste, and a few more items. When I was about to pay, I realized the money was not in my hands. I checked the floor around where I stood, and searched my food basket and pockets. The food money was missing! I returned to Mama in tears. Children who were wayward lost money, broke the bottles of milk they were sent to collect, or spent the money on candy to the disappointment and anger of parents. I was not one of those children. I had always been dependable.

Mama looked at the empty basket.

"Mama, I can't find the money," I said as I explained what had happened.

"Well it doesn't make sense to cry over spilled milk," she replied. "Wha I going do, kill yuh for eight dollars?"

I have no memory of how the household fared that week, but I remember I felt safe. Such was the feeling every time I transgressed, as all children do. Many years later when we recalled the incident together, I understood her humanity even more.

"Well, I lost my Grandie Sophie money a couple ah times!" Mama laughed, her familiar cooing sound jerking her belly.

CHAPTER TWENTY-ONE

Celebrating The Years

"Yuh never give me much trouble"

I COMPLETED HIGH School in 1972 and thereafter, I got my first job as a teacher. Teaching had always been a dream of mine, though at the time, I did not see the connection between my dream realized and Mama's dream deferred.

As a young teacher at the Greenbay Government School, the challenge was teaching students who were sometimes two years my junior. There was also the three-month wait to receive a first paycheck. I remember Mama's show of gratitude as I handed over fifty percent of the total amount to her. Tears did not flow, but I sensed a mutual acknowledgement that this was the first time I had been able to give back. Inside of me were tears of joy that the negative insinuations I had heard over the years, about my loyalty had never come to fruition. I felt proud.

Four years later, Mama beamed with pride at my graduation from the Teacher's Training College in Golden Grove Village. Years after, while I was in the British Virgin Islands on a two-year teaching contract, Mama came to visit with Shanara, one of her granddaughters. It was, for Mama, a much-needed vacation. She talked with my students who came by the house to meet her and she encouraged them to be serious about education and to aspire to be strong and independent women.

In 1982, I immigrated to America and attended college. By then most of Mama's family was living outside of Antigua. She visited New York City on a number of occasions to acquaint herself with a generation of grandchildren and great-grandchildren. One of Mama's visits to America was spent in Cleveland, Ohio with her grandson Byron, while he attended law school. Mama had raised him from since his mother left him at her gate, when he was but a few months old. Mama was a much-needed presence for his wife Carolyn as they experienced the birth of their first child, Shamfa. Mama assisted with the infant's care for a few months before returning to New York and eventually to Antigua. However, when Byron completed law school, his wish to have Mama at his graduation fell on deaf ears, for she was tired of traveling. She congratulated him by phone, explaining that her days of traveling to America had ended. Although it was a great disappointment to him, he understood. Being surrounded by grandchildren and family in America was good for her, but she missed sharing a chat with a neighbour across a fence. She always missed her garden at the house in Cassada Gardens, where she now resided, and the lack of tranquility in New York was difficult to adjust to at her seventy-odd years.

Mama's decision not to travel meant that the entire family had to find other ways to keep in contact. Each of us began making regular visits to Antigua. Some grandchildren were sent to join her household. Those who lived in other areas of Antigua, spent weekends and some holidays with her, experiencing the quality of parenting that was well known to those of us who were now grown.

One day my friend Everton remarked that it was very obvious how much I loved this woman. I was not aware that I spoke of her so often. For a long time it made me reflect truly on the depth of my love for her. I was pleased that he had recognized it. But that conversation also created some uncertainty. Did everyone who knew me realize how much I loved and appreciated Mama? I wanted to be sure. I decided that such a love needed to be proclaimed publicly, and so a plan incubated in my head. The year she turned seventy-nine, I returned to Antigua and hosted an evening with friends and family at my Cousin Eileen's home in Parham. It was a gathering to thank and acknowledge Mama for taking me from my father, for the love she had given to me over the years, and to let everyone know how much I loved her. It was an emotional moment for both of us as I read a special letter to her.

She said little at the end, but I knew that much more was said by her silence. "Yuh never gave me much trouble," was all she said. "Yuh were an easy child to raise."

The next year, on her eightieth birthday, her youngest son Barry, initiated plans to have a grand celebration of Mama May's life. A series of activities were planned, including a church worship service at the Anglican Cathedral, a picnic at the Runway Beach, a banquette at the Cultural Center, and a football match at King George V playgrounds. Hundreds of T-shirts were printed with Mama's picture on the front. All of her surviving children and almost all of her grand and great-grandchildren were present. That summer in Antigua will always be remembered as the time we celebrated the living, acknowledged all of Mama's work over the years, and let her know how much we appreciated and loved her.

Mama looked like an African queen the night of the banquet, dressed in a lavender two-piece suit and head wrap. She absorbed the well-deserved praises as she sat at a table flanked by her five surviving children: Ira, Barrymore, Pomroy, Elaine, and Fitzroy.

Mama was surrounded by friends and family and each speaker talked about her influence on their lives. I expressed my feelings for her, but my remarks were directed to the younger people. It was important for me that they show appreciation for her presence in their lives—that they understand the importance of Mama on a daily basis—that they respect and love her—that they learn as much as they could from her to pass on to their own children.

A year later, the first stroke occurred, summoning those of us abroad and around the island to Mama's bedside. She was eighty-one years old. The miraculous recovery left Mama's memory as sharp as a cutlass in sugar cane season.

Over the next three years, she looked forward to my visits and telephone calls. I taped our conversations as she shared information about her parents and neighbours, the times of both sadness and happiness. She loved to talk about her work, especially at the Fiennes Institute, where she was happiest taking care of the old and deprived. It seemed that a life of service to others was her purpose on this earth, and she was fully contented to have lived up to that task. We never ended a conversation without proclaiming our love for each other. She regularly inquired about my grandchildren Yahya, Khadeejah and Ahmad, and there was always a reminder to love and take care of them, that they were blessings from heaven and, so were precious gifts.

Over the years her penchant for writing letters never waned and I felt guilty many times over my lack of reciprocity. Her letters were filled with inquiries about others, about my well-being, and complaints about "the few old pains" she had. Most of all, she wrote that she was praying for everyone, and expressed her gratitude for monies sent in previous letters.

"The Lord bless you," she would say, in thanks for the many friends in Antigua: Mr. Roche, Gloria, Rhonda, Dudley, and Charles, all who would often visit to bring gifts.

Ira always returned to Antigua to celebrate her birthday, and Dave, Byron and his son Byron Jr., occasionally took time off to be there with her, too. The other children travelled home for visits at other times and many of the grandchildren like Quinton, Anthony, Kusa, Amardi, and Ibami, born overseas, spent summers with Mama. Whenever I was in Antigua, Mama and I would go for long drives and visit my Aunt Darling and cousin Eileen in Parham or cousins Eunette and Baby Dyer in John Hughes Village. Occasionally, we would stop for lunch either at the Grand Princess at Jolly Beach or Russell's at Fort James. Wherever we went, people treated Mama with a delicate and lovable attention. Humility radiated from her, inviting even more warmth and respect.

CHAPTER TWENTY-TWO

Fried Dumplings

"... Ah Making Journeycakes"

O VER THE YEARS of living in New York and traveling back and forth to Antigua, I have carried a host of West Indian foods back to America, including rum, bun and cheese, tea bush, and fried fish. I know that most of the items are in the Asian markets and bodegas around my neighbourhood in Ozone Park, but most Caribbean people would agree "them na taste de same." I had never brought johnnycakes before, but in 2003, a dozen of the fried dumplings were covertly packaged among the arsenal of treats bound for the Atlantic voyage. That day when the fried dumplings made the novelty journey from the V.C. Bird International airport under a smiling sun, I was reminded of the ubiquitous presence of johnnycakes during my childhood.

It had been two years since Mama had had her first stroke. Early on the morning I was to travel, she had called Gloria's house, where I was staying, and said, "Monica, ah making journeycakes for you to take back to the States."

At eighty-three, she was no longer cooking her own meals. Joyce her caregiver was doing an excellent job, but Mama would occasionally prepare a batch of the dumplings to not only slake our appetites, but also to prove to everyone that the old girl could still turn out an incomparable set.

Out of the blue, Mama decided that the dumplings should go to America.

Now, who would have thought that the innocuous-looking baked goods possessed even an iota of a threat to the safety of travelers? I could not imagine any Antiguan dish, be it pepper pot, doucana and salt fish, or shad and fungee, posing any kind of risk to passengers on a plane. But a meticulous and invasive check by a security guard at the airport opened my eyes to the possibility. The attack on the World Trade Center in New York and the Pentagon in Washington, DC in 2001 had brought us to this state where every little bottle of rum, bun and cheese, or winter green oil was potentially a weapon of mass destruction. The fingers of the security guard, which were fitted with acrylic nail extensions, moved like a tarantula through my suitcases.

"Ah ha, so wha in dis bag?" She asked. The emphasis was on "dis" as she squeezed a bag filled with buns. Mrs. Martin, who resided on Union Road, baked a special batch. It was custom for locals to give you something to take back to America.

"Buns," I replied. The guard was not a customs officer, but I felt a sense of authority from her anyway. This was just the check-in counter, and I imagined more searches at the Customs and in Puerto Rico, where I was scheduled to make my connection to New York. She surprised me, though, with the next question.

"Yuh have cheese, too?" She flashed a slight smile and two gold teeth sparkled in her mouth. I forced myself to respond because I wanted this unusual interrogation to end soon so that I could board the plane. I did not need all this attention.

Almost beneath my breath, I said, "Don't care for the salty cheese these days."

She looked at me as if to say, "Who eat bun without cheese?"

Mama's black plastic bag filled with johnnycakes now caught her attention. The guard's nails fumbled at the knot.

"So, wha in dis bag? Eh, eh, it even feels warm." I resisted making a response, but she stared brazenly at me. She wanted an answer even though she was already looking into the bag of warm dumplings.

Deliberately, I countered with a little American accent, "Just some journeycakes!"

"Cha, you mean fry bakes or fry dumplings man, ah who in God name call dem j-o-u-r-n-e-y cake?" she replied. Three gold chains dangled from her neck. A large pair of earrings swiveled below her ears.

I thought that if I gave her the history of the round dumplings, she might learn that although we were all West Indian, each island had its own history about certain foods. I wanted to tell her that they were, in fact, journeycakes, because centuries ago, in England they were a staple food taken on long trips, though they were much larger then.

However, I did not want to be too friendly. The guard was interfering with the cool, nonchalant attitude I consciously affected whenever I had to leave behind my Mama or my island. I had said goodbye to Mama fifteen minutes earlier and a knot was still in my chest. Though I visited regularly from New York, her parting remarks were always the same.

"So when ah going see yuh again before ah die?"

I would jokingly reply, "Mama, stop saying that; you not going anywhere."

The guard was relentless. "You mek dem you self, miss?" Eyeing me from my head to feet, she affirmed, "Cha, you nails look too fancy; you nah make them!"

Nobody made johnnycakes like Mama May, and she had been my teacher. Before I could talk, I had become familiar with the ingredients that went into creating top quality and tasty journeycakes. I passed flour, sugar, shortening, oil, baking powder, and salt to her with curiosity, wondering how she managed to balance the large bowl of dough in her lap as she punched it like a boxer, later forming golf balls to be flattened and fried.

The security guard continued, "You smart woman! You travel wid you own food! Dey no feed people good now on plane. De little puny sandwich just enough to stuff a toothache. Me, nowadays, I travel with me food too!"

No, this is not to eat on the plane. My son, Chiqui, loves fried dumplings. These are going straight to New York.

Now friendly, the guard's demeanour ate away at my pre-conceived notions about her. She said, "Gal, you good, good. Dats de kind a stuff you need to 'ave—dey even still warm and dey full belly."

By this time, the dumplings had unleashed an odor of oil and caused a few passengers to shift their heads in my direction.

Mama May's dumplings always grabbed attention. Long ago at picnics, everybody ate them: neighbours, bus drivers, even strangers on the beach.

Miss Chrissie, Mama's cousin, would say, "May, yuh fry dumplin' in a class by dey self."

Ms. Brookes, the neighbour, would ask, in a Kittitian accent, "How you dumpling pretty so, Miss May?"

Now I was proud to reply to the security guard, "My Mama just made them—I picked them up a few minutes ago." The guard reluctantly slid her hands from the package and closed the suitcase flap. I transferred the dumplings to my handbag, realizing they were too precious to leave in the suitcase.

"Well, miss, walk good, dat must be some loving Mama you 'ave dey." Her statement warmed my heart.

Looking through the window of the plane, the sky seemed infinitely white, filled with mountainous clouds textured like cotton balls. As we roared northward and left the sand and blue seas behind, nostalgia eased onto me again—another journey away from Antigua, and from Mama. Cupping my hands to my face, I inhaled the aroma of the dumplings on my fingers and smiled. The security guard must have the odor on her fingers too!

I thought of Mama as I had seen her earlier that morning. Two piles of dumplings surrounded her, as children buzzed about nearby.

I wondered if they had passed the ingredients to her as I did as a child. Back then, Mama squatted over a coal pot in the middle of the open yard and flipped the round dumplings with a fork, glowing with pride. She would confidently let me know, "Johnnycakes taste better cooked on coal fire anyway!"

On this day, the coal pot was inside the attached kitchen and there were no neighbours prying, no fragrance wafting over a galvanized fence, as there had been years ago. Now, the smell of fried oil permeated the air inside the house. It was the first greeting on entering the front door.

So I focused on the coal pot a few feet away from her. One pile, she said, was prettier, intended for the States, "Suitable for a journey overseas."

As I watched her pack them with care, thanking her for this unusual parcel, her gestures said much more. They transported me on a journey back into the past.

Growing up, when johnnycakes were made for Friday night's dinner, they were less about perfection. It was a time for creativity; it was a time to "cut and contrive" by stretching whatever ingredients were in the food safe.

"Dis is all Mama have tonight," she often said. Friday was also termed "...jury gone upstairs" time. We all knew what that meant: the food safe was bare, and so dinner was "weighing in the balance and found wanting," another of Mama's maxims that she used to trivialize difficult situations. We never cared about the absent jury, we just happily gulped down the floured dumplings followed by Kool-Aid or lemonade, and felt grateful.

Sometimes, with only flour to start, a few ingredients would be borrowed from a neighbour so that we could put a meal on the table. To any of us who seemed dissatisfied, Mama would say, "Mek out, be contented." And for the most part we were contented, for we ate affluently on Sundays, feasting on stewed chicken or meat stewed down with clove and browning, rice with peas, macaroni and cheese, sweet potatoes, and carrots. On these occasions, johnnycakes were just a side dish.

On Easter and Whit Mondays, the dumplings were made to ultimate perfection for picnics, because Mama's reputation was important.

"Put your best foot forward," was another one of her adages. Before dawn, as others turned in their beds for another hour's snooze, as cocks crowed around the neighbourhood, Mama's night's sleep would end. She would later unveil her masterpieces, which were wrapped in an embroidered cotton towel she had made herself. She shared johnnycakes with everyone.

On rainy days, johnnycakes were snuggly comfort food made on the spur of the moment. We used to huddle around Mama, sometimes dressed in her old frocks, and play with pieces of the dough. Sometimes, she would fry tiny dumplings for us to eat immediately. It was her way of saying to us, "I love you all." Of course, a full stomach was what we wanted and felt.

But these crispy fried dumplings were often filled with lessons. The joke round the house growing up was how Mama used johnnycakes to teach one of her sons, the young Jerome, not to steal. Jerome would constantly snatch our roasted corn or sneak money from her various hiding places. Such habits were becoming too pervasive, so Mama thought it was time to snap him out of it.

"Ah not raising no thief," she said to us. One day, she made johnnycakes, placing the first three finished cakes into a bowl covered with her usual embroidered towel. Shortly after, she added another three. She added another trio of johnnycakes, but then counted only seven in the bowl. She knew she wasn't crazy, nor did she need glasses.

She knew the little ones in the house would merely ask, "Give me a dumpling please, Mama," and she would either say, "take one," or "Wait till ah finish. Who you think ah making them for?"

Upon Jerome's next approach to the bowl, Mama eyed him. Her pupils rolled flush in the corners of each socket, while her head stared straight out at the coal pot of hot frying oil. It seemed that Mama was watching every tiny bubble that surrounded the dumplings as they changed into an edible brownness. With her pouting lips, she appeared to concentrate on the new piece of dough in hand as she tucked and rolled, tucked and rolled.

So, like a gentle breeze, Jerome floated toward Mama's back, gracefully folding his body in half and reached under the towel for a dumpling. Although Jerome was smart, he could not see those eye sockets, and could not believe that Mama could see the frying dumplings while her eyes were on the bowl of his targets. Mama, like a marksman, angled her fork towards the tilting towel.

"Yes, you want to be a thief?" she said. Jerome stood up to see the fork dangling in the skin of his hand, as if it were one of the dumplings being tested for doneness. He and Mama both screamed as the fork stood at attention on the back of his hand. Later, as Mama treated his wound with iodine and then bandaged it, she hoped the lesson had been learned. She felt some comfort amidst the guilt, as she was not going to raise any of her children as a thief.

Yes, johnnycakes snapped Jerome out of his crafty ways once and for all.

"Miss, would you like to have lunch?" It was the flight attendant, rousing me from my reminiscences. She placed a vegetarian offering on my tray table. The food barely cast a shadow. Instinctively, I opened the bag of journeycakes and shook my head as I got a whiff of the crust.

Putting four on my plate, I smiled and remembered the security officer saying, "Miss dey no feed people good on plane." I wondered if Mama knew this too? I weighed it all against my intention not to eat them on the plane. Helplessly, I devoured a few, savoring every bite just as I had so often done as a child.

As the delicate crust crumbled on top of my meager airline meal, my mind drifted again to Mama, seated at the coal pot that morning, packaging the dumplings for the American journey.

I realized that, like these journeycakes, I too was a package wrapped by her hands, chosen, mixed, kneaded and shaped. I hoped some of the grand and great-grandchildren who had waited for johnnycakes that morning would someday realize another ingredient in Mama's fried dumplings: the subliminal message of love.

CHAPTER TWENTY-THREE

Mama Is Hospitalized In 2006

"De Ole Girl Not Going Anyway Man"

IT WAS SUNDAY afternoon, February 19, 2006. Mama was back in hospital after suffering another slight stroke. Three of Mama's grandchildren—Byron, Andrea, Dave, and her daughter, Elaine, had recently returned to New York following another of Mama's brief hospital stays.

Ira, Elaine and I had arranged a meeting to discuss further long-term care for Mama, in anticipation of her release from hospital. Three o' clock that afternoon, driving from Queens to the Bronx to meet them, I received a second phone call from one of Mama's daughters-in-law, Sandy McPherson. She was like a daughter to Mama and assisted in her care over the years. Sandy was at the hospital in Antigua. Mama had a "turn for the worse," and we ought to come home to Antigua.

Sandy could not handle what was happening. I heard the sadness, fear, and alarm in her voice. Strangely, the previous day, Sandy had called me to say that Mama was talking and looked bright. My friends, Gloria and Elizabeth had visited Mama, too, and Mama told them that she knew I would be coming to see her when I got vacation in March. Mama knew spring break from my job at Allen Stevenson

School was approaching; she knew I had purchased a ticket and she knew the date I was to arrive. I was therefore convinced that since Mama was expecting me in March, everything was in order, she would be fine. However, I reasoned, *if she wanted me to come sooner, she would say so.* This was my mantra as I waited for spring to come.

Soon after I ended the phone call with Sandy, Byron called. I could hear the apprehension in his voice, for he had gotten a phone call from Sandy as well. What he said now made me happy. He would be coming to the meeting.

When I arrived at Elaine's home, I learned that Barrymore, Mama's youngest child, was also joining us. Minutes later, Ira knocked on the door. Immediately, I saw concern and trepidation in his eyes.

He headed straight to Elaine's living room couch and sat down.

"De old girl not going anyway, man. Mama strong," He sounded as if he needed confirmation. I wanted Ira to be right because I was not in Antigua. Spring break was weeks away. I was not at her bedside to caress her face, her belly and to tell her how much I love her. I was in an apartment in New York City, thousands of miles away from Mama. Thousands of miles away from the woman who had never ceased to love me. I comforted myself that she had bounced back in 2001. I needed her to hang on. Yes, we children never cease our demands on our parents; we continue to slice away at their sweetness, to suck every drop for our sustenance, believing it endless.

"Yes, Mama is strong. She was just talking on the phone with me few days ago." I said to Ira. Fear was slowly taking over my thoughts. I should have been in Antigua.

"I am going to Antigua tomorrow." I declared suddenly. Mama would hold on. I want to see her alive.

It took few minutes to reserve a seat on a flight out of Newark Liberty Airport the next day. Half an hour later, the phone rang. An eerie gloom descended upon the room. I picked up the receiver. It was a friend, Charles, who was at the hospital in Antigua. There were sounds of distant screams coming through the telephone. The screams were for Mama — she couldn't wait for spring break. I had planned to wait, knowing how strong she was, believing that "...de ole girl not going anywhere man."

It was the end of Mama May's reign, a culmination of her journey in this life. Though she was eighty-six years old, I had not conceived of the possibility of her death and was not prepared for it. Mama's influence even in death seemed to be at work, thousands of miles away, for what happened thereafter was an extraordinary indication of the force that defined her.

In about two hours, the apartment was filled with over thirty family members. There were all of Mama's surviving children — Elaine, Pomroy, Ira, Fitzroy, and Barrymore, many grandchildren, and great-grandchildren. They came from all parts of New York and New Jersey, drawn as if by a force and a will greater than themselves.

In that two-bedroom apartment in the Bronx, the many children God had placed into Mama's care cried together, and talked about her life. Like her journeycakes, all in the room were rolled and shaped by Mama May, just as Grandie Sophie had shaped her. Like journeycakes, she had been packaged to last for a long time. We knew, in our hearts, that her strength and commitment to family would influence the generations to come. For most of Mama's eighty-six years, she had given selflessly to so many. Like her dumplings, she was comfort food. She filled our hearts with love for all children and she created in us a yearning for better lives for our families. She taught us discipline towards work. She satisfied a hunger: not just a physical one, but one best characterized as a dedication to others. It was a journey never to be forgotten.

This poem was written as a tribute to Mama May by her grandson, Patrick Byron Tittle Esq. It was read at Mama's home-going celebration on March 6th 2006.

Tribute to an Angel

The Lord was taking attendance
of his chosen
for that sweet eternal sleep
amongst his angels
in the garden of eternal sleep
where the weeping willow never cries.

And I listened
but didn't hear your name
and, selfishly, I was happy
because I was not ready
for you to take that journey
a journey that is the natural consequence of life
failing to realize
that I was not meant to hear.

But, he must have called you by name
Because you answered
"present please"
with the enthusiasm of a child
on the first day of kindergarten
with a loving smile
and a spirit so at peace
as if to soothe my grief.

And yet, this grief has stricken me
I am numb from the sorrow and pain
never to be the same
because death
hath shook my very foundation
and plucked the leaves
making bare the first tree
in the peopled forest of my life.

Yet, I look upon your face
in this casket
this temporary place
and realize that this part of your journey
is not about me
but between you and your God
a road that you must trod.

Therefore, to truly honor your memory
I shall sit in silence
and watch as you quietly fly away
in the morning
And I shall wrap myself
in the comfort of your legacy
knowing that
although you leave this earth
with no earthly possessions
summoned back to your maker
from whence you came
You were RICH.

Material things you did not crave
CHARITY was your wealth
You had a profound effect on the lives you touched
and OH how you touched lives
leaving your everlasting print of love
compassion and unselfishness
embedded in our hearts, minds and souls.

From birth you were assigned a task
by God as a care-giver
and you have done the Lord's work
because you leave this earth
better than you found it
you have made a DIFFERENCE
in so many lives
and for that
you are richer than Kings.

A father to the fatherless
mother to the motherless
a friend in need
a friend indeed
a nurse for the sick
an ear for the depressed
a Hero
a Shero
a Teacher
the epitome of God's love and kindness
one of God's angels
my first love
the wind beneath my wings
and this world is a better place
because you were here Mama.

And now that God has called you home to rest
I shall not despair
because your life's lessons of love and compassion
shall sustain me here
in my heart and soul
and in each and everyone you have touched
we are fortunate to know you
we are blessed because of you.

And when the roll is called up yonder
your name will be there
the Lord will welcome you
his humble servant
with open arms and say
welcome home my child
JOB WELL DONE.